Breakdown and breakthrough

Breakdown and Breakthrough examines the essential role of regression in the patient's recovery from mental illness. In light of this, Nathan Field reassesses the role of the therapist, tracing psychotherapy back to its earliest spiritual roots and comparing modern analytic methods with ancient practices of healing and exorcism. The author uses vivid examples from his psychotherapeutic practice to show how, with the apparent breakdown of the therapeutic method itself, patients can break through to a new level of functioning.

The book goes on to consider how psychotherapy has been affected by fundamental developments in twentieth-century science, such as the move from old, classical assumptions of linear causation to non-linear complexity; from reductionism to a holistic-systems approach; from mental mechanisms to acknowledging the mysteries of unconscious interaction. Taking up the radical vision originally proposed by Carl Jung and later fostered by eminent psychotherapists such as Winnicott and Bion, the author shows how psychotherapy can be reframed to admit the existence of a psychological fourth dimension.

Nathan Field reappraises ideas of health and pathology, psychoanalysis and healing, sex and spirituality in light of a dramatic shift in the way we understand ourselves. How this shift alters the shape of psychotherapy in the twenty-first century is the challenge that practitioners, teachers and trainees must all address.

Nathan Field is an Analytical Psychotherapist with over thirty years' experience. He works in private practice in London.

Breakdown and breakthrough

Psychotherapy in a new dimension

Nathan Field

London and New York

First published 1996
by Routledge
11 New Fetter Lane, London EC4P 4EE

Simultaneously published in the USA and Canada
by Routledge
29 West 35th Street, New York, NY 10001

© 1996 Nathan Field

Typeset in Palatino by Routledge
Printed and bound in Great Britain by
TJ Press Ltd, Padstow, Cornwall

British Library Cataloguing in Publication Data
A catalogue record for this book is available from the British
Library

Library of Congress Cataloguing in Publication Data
Field, Nathan, 1924–
    Breakdown and breakthrough: psychotherapy in a new
    dimension /Nathan Field
    p. cm.
    Includes bibliographical references and index.
    1. Regression (Psychology)—Therapeutic use. 2. Psycho-
    analysis.
    I. Title
    RC489.R42F54 1996
    616.89'14—dc20   96–5997
                                                                CIP

ISBN 0–415–10957–4 (hbk)
ISBN 0–415–10958–2 (pbk)

To Sheila, with love

Contents

Acknowledgements

I wish to acknowledge a debt of gratitude to my patients whom it has been a privilege and a challenge to know; and to the editors of the *British Journal of Psychotherapy* and the *Journal of Analytical Psychology* in whose pages some of the material included in this book first appeared.

Chapter 1

Interpreting and relating

Soon after I qualified as a psychotherapist a man was referred to me suffering from depression. His reason for seeking help was an acute anxiety that his fiancée no longer wished to marry him. In his sessions we explored both his current and past relationships to see if there was a common pattern whereby the people he cared about sooner or later came to reject him; and in particular why he felt so devastated at the prospect of his engagement ending.

In fact, it ended soon after, but Malcolm (as I shall call him) kept coming in order to help work through the loss. He was a touchy man who sometimes irritated me, but he was essentially warm, had a wry sense of humour, and I soon came to like him. After two years he felt sufficiently improved to consider leaving. In preparation for this we reviewed what benefit he had got from coming: there had been no dramatic transformations but he had survived his rejection, he felt considerably more alive, and seemed to have emerged from a depression that had apparently lain on him since adolescence. On the whole it was an acceptable outcome. Then he added:

'Oh, and one more thing. My sex problem cleared up.'

I was baffled.

'What sex problem? I never knew you had one.'
'Yes. Well...I suffered from...premature ejaculation ever since I
    could remember. Always, actually.'
'But you never once mentioned it?'
'No, I suppose I didn't. I was getting round to telling you, but it
    actually cleared up by itself in the first few months.'
'But we never talked about it?'

'No we didn't. That's true. Strange, isn't it?'

It was indeed strange and proved to be one of many experiences encountered in my clinical work that I could not readily explain. My training as an analytical psychotherapist led me to assume that I would be treating people suffering from a psychological illness whose cure lay in the analysis of their problems. My task was primarily to listen and, at the appropriate time, to offer interpretations that would help them understand their psychic conflicts:

> The role of the analyst is confined to interpreting the patient's material, and all criticism, advice, encouragement, reassurance and the like, is rigorously avoided. The interpretations are centred on the transference situation, impartially taking up manifestations of positive and negative transference as they appear.
>
> (Segal 1986: 3)

This approach follows Freud's original recommendation that analysis should be carried out in a state of abstinence, that the analyst should scrupulously avoid either gratifying or criticising the patient and should maintain an attitude of benevolent neutrality. The rationale of presenting the patient with a 'well polished mirror', of quite deliberately avoiding being 'human', is that it provides a situation whereby the patient's idiosyncratic ways of relating can be clearly observed and interpreted. The most effective interpretations are those that focus on the relationship between patient and analyst, since they demonstrate that the ways in which the patient reacts to the analyst are based on defensive childhood patterns that are no longer applicable to adult life and can therefore be given up. If the analyst, in his or her urge to heal, acts in any way to excite either the patient's love or hatred, this contaminates the situation and robs interpretations of objectivity and conviction.

In his advice to future analysts Freud quoted with approval the remark of a celebrated military surgeon who said: 'I bind the wounds, God heals them' (1912). The implication is that it is not the analyst's job to heal but at best to create the conditions for healing; that it would be presumptuous of the analyst to attempt to do so and an indication that he or she had been seduced by the patient's expectations. The analyst's job is limited to clarifying the patient's inner conflicts in order that the patient will be able to solve his or her problems.

While the setting and regularity of the analytic relationship had always been acknowledged to provide the necessary stable environment in which this could take place, Freud was careful not to make things too cosy for the patient (1919). Through the 'rule of abstinence' he ensured that the dynamic of the analytic endeavour would not be sabotaged by mere gratification. Freud took the broadly masculine view that if an indulgent mother keeps spoon-feeding her baby, the child just won't make the effort to feed himself. For Freud love, in the form of positive transference, was valuable only in so far as it held the patient in the treatment while the process of unmasking the id went on. It was never regarded as a therapeutic agent in its own right. Indeed, it could become a serious obstacle if the patient, instead of remembering his or her infantile attachments, attempted to re-enact them. By the same token, if the analyst, instead of restricting him or herself to interpretation, endeavoured to compensate for the deficiencies of the patient's original parents, that would be an unwarranted presumption and doomed to fail.

The vast literature on transference and countertransference, while never denying the importance of the patient–therapist relationship, in fact rarely describes it in a straightforward manner. With few exceptions, the phobic anxieties around countertransference result in a jargon-ridden, pseudo-scientific language of mental mechanisms. Even in the papers of Fairbairn (1952) and Guntrip (1968), the analyst's care and love are never openly acknowledged. Balint, whose touch seems more human, rarely gives us a glimpse of how things really felt inside his consulting room, beyond conceding that when the patient is nearing the 'area of basic fault' the atmosphere can become 'highly charged' (Balint 1958). Love, with its ever present threat of sex, seems the major taboo, whereas rage and contempt are far more frequently described as they are presumably safer to handle.

The rival claims of indulgence and abstinence, each represented by Freud's two chief lieutenants, Ferenczi and Abraham, go back to the earliest years of the psychoanalytic movement. The latter strongly advocated that neurotics will only grow out of their original state of narcissism if they learn to bear the pain of deprivation, and this has come to characterise the classical analytic attitude. Ferenczi constantly experimented with methods of shortening the treatment. One of these was his relaxation technique which involved creating a benign, regressive environment the patient could sink into:

> The extent to which patients improved when I employed this relaxation-therapy in addition to the older method (frustration) was in many cases quite astonishing ... after we had succeeded in a somewhat deeper manner than before in creating an atmosphere of confidence between physician and patient, and in securing a fuller freedom of affect, hysterical physical symptoms would suddenly make their appearance, often for the first time in an analysis extending over years.
>
> (Ferenczi 1955: 118)

Ferenczi's conviction that the therapist's love is vital to improvement involved him in occasionally embracing his patients, or taking them on holiday with him. In the case of his patient Elizabeth Severn he even experimented with his becoming *her* patient for a time (Stanton 1990). It was as if he was prepared to try every possible way to create that primary trust which he considered indispensable to the healing process.

Fearful that Ferenczi's excesses would damage the reputation of psychoanalysis, Freud reluctantly withdrew his support, which Ferenczi found a devastating personal blow. Although his challenge to the rule of abstinence proved a failure, the question of providing a warm, positive environment, so closely identified with the mothering role, still remains an issue in therapeutic technique. The British School of Object Relationship analysts, led by Winnicott and Balint, espoused a markedly more maternal tone: softer, more flexible, sometimes even playful. While never denying the power of interpretation – indeed themselves masters of the art – they increasingly emphasised the importance of holding. This was intended in the metaphorical sense of 'holding in mind', but it reflected the importance of a pre-verbal, mother–baby relationship. Balint was very explicit that there are phases in the therapy when the patient regresses to a stage where the therapist is required to adopt an altogether different approach; not one of interpretation, which makes no sense at this level, but of simple attunement (Balint 1968).

The unverbalised, containing relationship on the one hand and the insight-promoting interpretation on the other would appear to constitute a pair of opposites. Balint recommends the first as appropriate in states of regression, the second when the therapeutic alliance has been established. They stand in the same relationship to one another as figure and ground, or structure and process, or maleness and femaleness, logos and eros. Whether they complement or conflict with one another is an unresolved dialectic that runs all through this book.

The dialectical way of addressing phenomena was especially characteristic of Jung in that almost every one of his leading ideas is presented in terms of opposites which balance each other, albeit that balance may be very difficult to achieve.

> For Jung, bipolarity is of the essence; it is a necessary condition for psychic energy and for a life lived at a level other than that of blind instinctuality. Opposites are required for the definition of any entity or process – one end of a spectrum helps to define the other, to give us a conception of it.
>
> (Samuels 1985: 92)

With the accumulation of clinical experience Freud came to realise that psychological illness was far more resistant than he had originally thought. As he encountered each new area of difficulty he made intriguing new discoveries, but over time came increasingly to regard psychoanalysis less as a form of treatment and more as a unique tool of research into the human psyche. In this respect his achievement has been immense. Through his method of interpreting dreams he became the first to recognise that the unconscious has its own laws. His use of the analytic setting, combined with his unique method of listening, constitutes a discovery of the profoundest significance. He recommended that the analyst adopt an attitude of 'evenly hovering attention' whereby he frees his mind of all preconceptions, expectations, judgements and even focus; otherwise 'there is danger of never finding anything but what is already known' (Freud and Breuer 1895: 324). What Freud advocates is a sort of primeval vision that lies at the root of all discovery. By means of unfocused attention, which actually requires a process of unlearning, the analyst can more readily identify the patient's unconscious conflicts. It is the expectation of psychotherapy that if these can now be made conscious the outcome will be a reduction of neurotic suffering. In my experience this did frequently happen. As certain patients gained insight they progressively improved; in some cases even a blindingly obvious interpretation produced quite dramatic benefits; although on the whole improvement occurred in small cumulative increments which became evident only on looking back over a period of time.

TWO PATTERNS OF CHANGE

But I had other cases where things did not turn out in quite this way. Especially disturbing were those where, in spite of the most carefully thought out interpretations, my patients didn't seem to make real progress. Each gain seemed to get cancelled out by a relapse, and eventually we would reach a state of impasse where I felt I had exhausted every possible interpretation and had nothing new to offer. With the deepest reluctance I would become convinced that this particular patient would have a better chance with someone else and decided to take it up with them at the very next session.

But a surprise was in store. My patient would arrive saying the deadlock was over, in fact they had never felt more hopeful.... It was almost as if they had heard my private thoughts and pre-empted my decision to abandon them. The treatment would continue from that point in a much more positive manner. This cycle of events happened on a number of occasions; that is, we reached a state of breakdown, which was followed by an unexpected breakthrough, possibly followed much later by another breakdown, and so on. This pattern frequently occurred within a single session: a patient might talk in a particularly driven way, undeterred by my attempts to make contact, until eventually I would entertain the thought: 'It's just not going to work today...' and stop trying – at which point the atmosphere mysteriously changed and our dialogue became meaningful.

Since there was no specific reason why a prolonged deadlock should suddenly lift, apart from my private decision to give up, I began to think there might be a link between breaking down and breaking through. It seemed that some patients could not take a genuine step forward without reaching the end of their tether; and this invariably meant that I had reached the end of mine. I now began to consider if there were two patterns of change: the first continuous, progressive and incremental; the second discontinuous and cyclic in that it followed an alternating pattern of 'progression-regression-progression'. Instead of simply building on what had gone before there seemed to occur a disintegration of previous achievement, followed by a gratifying jump to a new level of functioning. A characteristic example occurred with my patient Elaine.

When Elaine first came to see me she was in her forties, married, and the mother of two children. She recalled her childhood as massively restricted, thanks to her overprotective mother and a strict Catholic upbringing. With this went a persistent sense of inferiority towards her twin sister who did much better at school and who, due to a variety of childhood illnesses, also succeeded in gaining most of their mother's attention. Very early on in life Elaine learnt that it paid to be ill. She must have been a difficult, angry child, a slow developer who performed badly at school but was actually filled with energies and capacities no one even began to recognise.

All through her teens she longed to get away from home and, in her early twenties, she met a young man who wanted much the same. He had grown up as the youngest son in a joyless household of controlling women and, although pampered, he too sought escape. Each seemed the answer to the other's need and they looked forward to a wonderful new life together. During their engagement her fiancé became diabetic, but this only evoked in Elaine a self-sacrificing readiness to devote her life to his care. 'Even if he lives just a few years,' she thought, 'I shall have given him some happiness.' At this time a devoted Catholic, she harboured secret aspirations to saintliness; but she reckoned without her very quick temper and resentment at being exploited. In this respect, she disastrously overestimated her own capacities for self-sacrifice: her husband lived for another thirty years and neither one gave the other much happiness in all that time.

Sexual difficulties emerged immediately on marriage and, in spite of desperate efforts on both sides, were never overcome. It became a source of deep disappointment to both, but Elaine took all the blame. A few months after marriage her father died; within weeks she was in a state of severe breakdown and became an in-patient in a mental hospital where she remained for the next eighteen months. Instead of Elaine looking after her diabetic husband, he found himself obliged to look after her.

The years that followed were filled with tension and bitterness, guilt and failure. Each was a profound disappointment to the other and to themselves; each was the victim of expectations neither could fulfil. It was all the sadder when one remembers the hopes with which this marriage began. But the one positive aspect was that, from their few attempts to have a sexual life, their two daughters were born, and the love each partner found so difficult to show the other became invested in their children. It was very likely a repeat of what had happened with their own parents.

In clinical terms Elaine's pathology covered a broad spectrum of disturbance: almost continuous anxiety; phases of depression and even depersonalisation; considerable paranoia; constant splitting with an excessive use of projective identification. Subjectively she had a chronic sense of 'wrongness': she was either 'not there' or 'too much', either a victim or a bully. Mostly angry or depressed, but sometimes quite manic, she spent most of her time regretting the past or longing for a better future. Her mind was hardly ever in the present. Everything seemed to hit her 'on the raw': it was as if she lacked normal ego-filters and could not defend herself against an excess of stimuli. I began to realise that her sexual frigidity arose not from a lack of sexual responsiveness but an excess of it. If she felt loving she could barely control her erotic excitement; if her anger was aroused she felt she could vomit or defecate. What looked like frigidity was a chronic over-reaction against her excessive somatisation of tender or excited feelings. All her energies were expended into trying to keep them in control; as a result she was massively self-conscious and could hardly ever 'be herself'. The chief agent of control was her GP who she visited frequently and who maintained her on a regular dosage of tranquillisers, anti-depressants and other drugs.

When the following session took place Elaine had been coming to see me for several years; from the moment she entered the room she flooded me with bitter remarks about everyone in her life. This was not uncommon, she always had a grievance to offload, but in this particular session her flow of criticism was unusually sustained. Although I was not personally included I had an uncomfortable feeling of being attacked. She continued in this vein for over half the session, rounding off with a complaint that since she lived in a 'dead end' her neighbours repeatedly backed their cars into her driveway and poisoned her with exhaust fumes. Having several times failed to break into her monologue, I finally speculated aloud that perhaps she was now discharging that poison right now? She replied: 'It's not my imagination, you know. They do it all the time.' I did not persist but found it very 'dead end' that she refused to shift from concrete facts to any exploration of her present feelings. It was like talking to someone locked in a bad dream. In retrospect my observation about discharging her poison, although voiced in a neutral manner, hid my growing anger. I did not know it at the time, but she had succeeded in pouring her aggression into me and I had become the receptacle for a massive quantity of projective identification. Both her rage and her sense of impotence were beginning to take me over, because by now I had the alarming experience of being virtually unable to think. A dreadful void seemed to have opened up in my head, yet at the same time it seemed clogged with chaotic thoughts. I felt awful but dared not reveal what was happening and just kept silent. Elaine found my continuing silence very frightening but it served to mask my mounting panic, as well as my unconscious retaliation for her attack. As the silence persisted the tension between us kept growing.

Eventually Elaine managed to say: 'Look, I feel a bit queer. Rather faint actually. It's a kind of "nothing" feeling, just like I used to get before my breakdown.' I looked at her, quite unable to say anything, just struggling with my own unbearable 'nothing' feeling. With increasing urgency she went on: 'Actually I feel I'm breaking to pieces. . . . Please, please say something. . . . Why can't you talk? *Why can't you just say something?*'

I could see the blood had drained from her face and the perspiration was showing on her upper lip. I could hear her telling me she was reliving the breakdown she had suffered some years before and was begging me not to leave her alone in it. In a profoundly counter-therapeutic sense I was sharing it: my mind, like hers, was utterly blank and my whole being filled with dread. I knew that I could only begin to talk again by admitting the state I was in, but this seemed tantamount to admitting my breakdown as a psychotherapist. At the same time I had the conviction that I really had to respond. I knew that if I didn't confess my help-lessness and continued to remain silent, something really destruc-tive would happen. With the distinct feeling that I was committing professional suicide I managed to utter: 'The fact is, I can't speak.' She looked at me. I wasn't sure if she had heard me or took in what I said. I repeated: 'It's not that I won't speak. I *can't*.' Elaine blinked, then she looked away and began to cry. Within moments I knew the crisis was over. She recognised, either by my words or my look, that I had some inkling of how her breakdown had felt, and instead of rejecting me as useless she suddenly looked very grateful and vulnerable.

What followed was an unexpected, unforgettable event. It consisted of about a minute of silence; not the agonised silence we had both previously endured but a brief intercession of quiet joy. It was not ecstatic but extraordinarily calm and precise. I had the clearest sense of being intimately in touch with Elaine yet quite separate; somehow deeply connected with her yet more myself than I had ever been. I have no doubt that for Elaine it was the same.

How did we contrive to switch from a state of alienation to rapport? On reflection, Elaine had succeeded in inducing in me, through the process of projective identification, the paranoid-schizoid state she herself was in. I only understood this later when I had partly succeeded in struggling free of it; while I was possessed by it I had no reference point to tell me I was in it. My failure to resist or contain it was evidenced by my helpless silence, and this only served to intensify it in both of us. It was an event my training was expressly designed to avoid, but the unconscious proved wiser than my professional ego. Although it rendered me speechless, although confessing my impotence felt like jumping off a cliff, I nonetheless knew that I had a responsibility not to push her into another breakdown. So I gave up. But I suppose I gave up only my professional ego, not my professional commitment. In the moment that Elaine grasped that I was in the same state as herself she no longer felt alone and her tears were tears of profound relief. Seeing me truly defenceless I think she was enabled to let go of her own defences and we briefly entered into what was virtually a state of communion.

Although the intimacy of our silence frightened her and she broke it after a short while, it was her first experience of being simply and serenely herself, free of her chronic self-consciousness. It would seem to have marked the beginning of a profound change in her inner life, as I gradually realised that her bitter litanies of reproach against others and herself were diminishing. This was an intriguing observation: much as she complained of the torments that everyday life brought her she dared not renounce them. It was as if she were addicted to misery, guilt and anger; they were the feelings her mother had evoked in her all through her childhood and without her mother's controlling presence she felt unsafe. To feel at peace she had to relinquish watchful self-control; but without control she felt like an 'abandoned woman' and that was the same as becoming an abandoned child.

Her fear of peace came in various guises: if she did not speak I would find her boring, or if she did not produce problems for me to solve I would send her away. Sometimes the silences became unbearably intense, either because she felt cut off from me, or so suffocatingly close to me that she felt herself choking. But being comfortable together brought its own problems: sensing that I held her in mind, it was as if I held her in my arms and she could not cope with being sexually aroused. Behind this was an even greater dread: in a state of rapport it was as if her very identity was melting away. Only anger or guilt could restore her familiar sense of a separate self, and so she quickly returned to her storehouse of grievances. But over time her capacity to cope with phases of quiet connectedness increased, although we never again reached the spontaneous rapport of that first occasion.

Almost a year later, during a particularly depressed session, I asked Elaine if it had been worth coming to therapy all this time?

She said: 'Yes.'
I persisted: 'Yet your life seems as fraught and painful as ever?'
She replied: 'That may be. But now I'm a person, and that's what really counts.'

Chapter 2

Breakdown and breakthrough

I have suggested there might be two patterns of psychological change. The first I described as linear and progressive, the second as more complex in that it followed a cyclic pattern of breakdown–breakthrough. Although manifestly different, both processes could be seen to complement one another, in so far as every therapy would appear to involve some measure of regression interspersed with phases of steady progress.

The notion of 'getting worse before you can get better' is hardly new; the equivalent in French is *'reculer pour mieux sauter'*, going back in order to leap forward. In physical medicine every doctor knows that a fever must reach its peak, after which things may go either way. This goes back to the ancient Greeks who recognised the healing pattern of *crisis* followed by *lysis*. In mythology it is symbolised by the phoenix rising from the ashes. Jung noted that any extreme tends to evoke its opposite, a process he called *enantiodromia*, a term originally used by the ancient Greek philosopher Heraclitus. In his view the tension of opposites is self-compensatory: a bright light produces a strong shadow. It was one of his basic convictions that the psyche is a self-regulating organism. The unconscious will naturally balance consciousness although it may reach the severity of a breakdown.

One especially serious manifestation of breakdown can be seen in clinical depression. It is serious because it can last a lifetime and end in suicide. Depression is generally regarded, all too understandably, in a profoundly negative light. Jung took a less pessimistic view. He had himself gone through a profound personal depression after his split with Freud (as did Ferenczi, who died not long after), but his most original discoveries came out of this breakdown and his capacity to recover from it.

A number of other Jungian writers have taken a similarly open-ended view, the most recent being David Rosen in his book *Transforming Depression* (1993). As part of his medical training Rosen chose to interview those few individuals who had survived a suicide leap from the Golden Gate Bridge in San Francisco.

The ten survivors gave various reasons for jumping, but there was a common core feeling of aloneness, alienation, depression, rejection, worthlessness and hopelessness. Although the ten had widely divergent views of religion before attempting suicide, they all admitted to feelings of spiritual transcendence after they had leaped.

(Rosen 1993: xxii)

Rosen's approach to treating severe depression, based on the Jungian view that breakdown can be understood as the psyche's attempt at self-healing, is to make every effort to shift the actual *suicidal* urge towards what he calls *egocide*. This is the name he gives to the renunciation of a particular personal ideal, such as being a good mother, a successful businessman, a brave soldier, etc., which hitherto had made life meaningful. Rosen recounts how he himself, in his student days, was driven near suicide through the failure of his marriage. He came slowly to relinquish his particular ideal of what constituted a satisfactory husband. This amounted to his entering into a voluntary breakdown over a long and painful period, but the result was a major developmental transformation.

The same process applies in every therapy: each patient arrives with his particular ego formation, originally forged out of his personal experience of life: the deep impress, that is, of the family and world he grew up in. What he needs to learn is to adapt to the world he lives in now, which involves the modification of his archaic, maladapted ego structure. By modification I mean a bit-by-bit breaking down of the old ego so that new bits, better adapted to reality, can grow in their place. This is made easier by the process of regression that the therapy situation induces: by reverting to the more malleable, trusting ego of the child there can be a melting-down, rather than a breaking-down. But too easy a melting-down is also suspect, because it is unlikely to endure. The rebel recruit who takes the longest to 'break' usually proves the toughest soldier. A word like breakdown carries powerful connotations, but I intend the term to apply to any of the myriad instances when the ego fails to function, such as the moment when we forget to put a name to a familiar face or become tongue-tied. It is commonly acknowledged that the harder we try the worse it gets and eventually we are forced to give up. This is actually the moment of breakdown; presently, after we have forgotten the problem, the name or thought we had so desperately sought will quietly come to mind. It is as if we had been pushing at a door that opens inwards. An important principle is at stake here, a type of psychological judo which lies at the root of the psychotherapeutic method. One of the commonest exchanges in therapy occurs when the analyst makes a clarifying interpretation which the patient really grasps. For example, the analyst says: 'Can you see that in this instance, as in many others, you contrive to make yourself a victim?' The patient stops to take this in, then responds: 'Yes, I do see...yes that's right...that fits,' and then follows with: 'Then what do I *do*?' To which the analyst unsatisfactorily replies: 'You can't do anything. You just understand it.'

To be told you can't do anything is to be rendered impotent; to the extent the patient accepts this, accepts that he or she cannot by conscious action stop being a habitual victim, he or she suffers an interior breakdown. But only from this point can change take place. The same shift occurs in the therapist. Only when we therapists can admit that we cannot understand, only when we stop persuading ourselves that we do understand, can understanding come of itself. The essence is a giving up of something and it cannot be pre-empted. We have to keep trying and give up only when we are forced to; to try not to try is still trying.

DIVERSE FORMS OF BREAKDOWN AND BREAKTHROUGH

What I have termed the breakdown–breakthrough pattern can, in fact, be observed across a vast spectrum of existence far beyond the human and personal. The historian Toynbee traced the same pattern in the collapse and rise of whole civilisations. Over the centuries they become top heavy, with an increasingly rigid bureaucracy and an oppressive aristocracy, eventually provoking a revolution from below. More often, they are invaded by 'barbarians' who set up a new regime – only to go through the same process themselves in the fullness of time. If the invaders are successfully repelled the crisis may, like those failed suicides described above, initiate a new and more viable social system and so the society will have renewed itself for another period of time (Toynbee 1972).

These are the societies that rise and fall and rise again in what Robert Hinshelwood (1988) calls a 'sinusoidal' pattern. He traces it in the history of institutions, taking as an example the therapeutic community. Some he terms as having 'bounce' – they have their highs and their lows but manage to survive. Others, after a spectacular period of growth, simply 'fall flat' and never recover. This may have been prompted by the death of the charismatic leader who founded the organisation. He describes a situation where, once the decline has set in, it becomes all but impossible to reverse it: the organisation has fallen into a 'demoralisation trap'.

What properties does the organisation with bounce possess that the one that falls flat does not? Which factors, that is, provide a positive way out from the state of breakdown? This is a crucial question for both organisations and individuals. Hinshelwood presents the demoralised organisation as trapped like a surfer under a collapsing wave: there is no way he can surf directly up and over the top. Given the current state of world affairs, in which the widespread breakdown of civilised norms in combination with hitherto unprecedented powers of destruction have led to genocide and relentless ecological destruction, it might be legitimately inferred that the greater part of human society is presently caught in a demoralisation trap.

However, Hinshelwood suggests that a surfer might find an escape by following an upward path along the *cusp* of the wave, provided they can move faster than the wave collapses behind them. I find it of significance that, basing his solution on ideas from chaos theory, Hinshelwood shifts from a two- to a three-dimensional model, a recourse I explore in greater depth later on.

The same regression–progression pattern applies to the evolutionary development of living forms. The biologist Garstang termed it paedomorphosis, a process whereby evolution itself can be seen to proceed by retracing its steps, as it were, along the path which led to the dead end and making a fresh start in a more promising direction (see Koestler 1967: 163–9). The human species, for example, is an offshoot not of the fully developed ape, but of the ape embryo: it was from this malleable half-formed stage that human stock emerged. Koestler notes that the same pattern applies to the evolution of ideas:

The revolutions in the history of science are successful escapes from blind alleys. The evolution of knowledge is continuous only during those periods of consolidation and elaboration which follow a major break-through. Sooner or later, however, consolidation leads to increasing rigidity, orthodoxy, and so into the dead end of overspecialisation. . . . Eventually there is a crisis and a new 'break-through' out of the blind alley, followed by another period of consolidation, a new orthodoxy, and so the cycle starts again.

(Koestler 1967: 168)

At the personal level the breakdown–breakthrough pattern can be observed in most accounts of the creative process. There is abundant documentation how scientists such as Einstein, Kekulé or Poincaré wrestled for years with an intractable problem until they virtually gave up – and were then presented with the solution in a doze! The entire scenario of *The Rite of Spring* ballet came to Stravinsky in a dream. The psychoanalyst, Marion Milner, describes the process as follows:

the inescapable condition of true expression was the plunge into the abyss, the willingness to recognise the moment of blankness and extinction was the moment of incipient fruitfulness, the moment without which the invisible forces within could not do their work.

(Milner 1987: 5)

A possible explanation of how this may come about can be found in the physiology of the brain. This comprises three levels: the reptilian 'old brain' known as the diencephalon which emerges from the spinal column; this is overlaid by the mid-brain where the thalamus is located; and uppermost, the bicameral cortex whose special development is unique to the human species. Our rational faculties would appear to be directly related to the cortex. When these fall into abeyance through sleep, the activity of the subcortical zones comes into awareness as dreams, and would seem to be the source of creative inspiration.

In the brief phase before the onset of sleep, and before fully awakening, there may also occur what is known as a waking dream. A considerable number of people can induce it at will by voluntary relaxation; in this twilight state random phrases, voices, images, music, faces, even elaborate dream-like scenes, all appear with a heightened intensity of sound and colour (Mavromatis 1987). These hypnagogic images are singular in that neuroscientific research indicates they do not actually use the visual pathways associated with the cortex but emerge directly from the old and mid-brain centres. These follow quite different laws from those of the cortex, just as dreams follow different laws from waking consciousness. It would make sense to hypothesise that, once the cortex is temporarily de-activated, the solution to a previously insoluble problem can be grasped directly by the subcortical centres, usually in a pictorial form, which was how Einstein and Kekulé experienced it. Truly creative solutions seem to emanate from these so-called lower centres, although they need the prior stimulation of intense and prolonged conscious effort.

One startling implication of this research suggests that, in all likelihood, sub-cortical activity goes on continually; that is, we are *always dreaming*, day and night, but only become aware of it when consciousness is laid to rest in sleep. This is analogous to the fact that the stars shine both by day and night, but they only become visible when their light is no longer drowned out by the glare of the sun.

BREAKDOWN AND BREAKTHROUGH IN RELIGIOUS LIFE

The breakdown–breakthrough pattern can also be clearly traced in biographical records of the major figures in religious history. Nearly all of them report passing through phases of profound despair before reaching the spiritual peace they sought. St John's 'dark night of the soul' is one of the best known examples. In clinical terms he went through a prolonged depression which, with immense courage and determination, he consciously used to strip away all ego and all desire, including the desire even for those spiritual gratifications he felt God had once given him. By doing so, he came out the other side into the radiant centredness that characterises the liberated individual.

In his classic study *Varieties of Religious Experience*, William James (1901) presents case after case of individuals who, like several of my own patients, had to reach the very end of their tether before they could find salvation. Many of James's examples are drawn from the Christian evangelical tradition where the eloquence of the preacher succeeded in reducing members of their congregation to abject repentance – whereafter they flung themselves onto the 'mercy of God' and found deliverance. This worked especially well in temperance meetings with those alcoholics who were already deep into despair. The preacher effectively acted as a group exorcist. By terrifying reminders of sin and threats of hell-fire he rapidly brought about the death of the 'old Adam' so that the 'new Adam' could be born. In each successful case there was a permanent giving up of the existing ego, whether it be that of a persistent drunkard or, at quite another level, the blamelessly devout St John.

The same abreactive dynamics are currently at work in the dramatic phenomena, such as the Toronto Blessing, that occur at Christian charismatic meetings:

> At the climax, two lines of believers wound from the ground to the first floor balcony above, where pastors blessed them. Almost every last participant was 'slain in the spirit' and fell down. It was an unforgettable picture.
>
> (Cotton 1996)

Just as the stage hypnotist can successfully work with only the most suggestible of his volunteers and dismisses the remainder, so those believers who collapse, speak in tongues or howl like dogs at charismatic gatherings are self-selected. They are by temperament highly suggestible individuals and often going through a phase of intense personal stress:

> In five years of talking with born-again Christians for 'The Hallelujah Revolution', my book about religious revival, I lost count of the times they recounted histories of deep depression.
>
> (Cotton 1996)

The breakdown–breakthrough pattern fits particularly well with the Christian faith since its founder was himself reported to have gone through the same process: a painful death followed by a miraculous resurrection. Two earlier gods, the Greek Dionysus and the Egyptian Osiris suffered the same fate of death and resurrection, with the additional detail that each was dismembered and later reassembled in a transfigured form. It is interesting to note that this feature of dismembering followed by re-membering, albeit in dreams or visions, is a common element in the training of the shaman (Eliade 1964).

Zen Buddhism grasps the same point very clearly. Nearly all its teaching stories seek to illustrate how the existing self acts as an impediment to change. A charming example describes the university professor who visited the master Nan-in to learn about Zen. Nan-in served tea. He poured his visitor's cup full – and still kept on pouring. The professor watched his cup overflowing until he protested: 'It is already overfull. No more will go in.' 'Like this cup,' said Nan-in, 'you are full of your own opinions and speculations. How can I show you Zen unless you first empty your cup?' (Reps 1971).

The emptying of the cup is the aim of the Zen 'koan' system of spiritual training. The aspirant is given an inherently insoluble conundrum, such as 'What is the sound of one hand clapping?', and told to solve it. He or she offers one ingenious answer after another, and each is rejected. With each rejection the student becomes ever more baffled but is instructed to concentrate still harder. The student wrestles with the problem night and day, until he or she loses all capacity to think his or her way through it (Kapleau 1967). There exists a book which gives the 'correct' answer to each koan, but in practice the answers are irrelevant. The aim of the training is to drive the student to such a degree of desperation that he or she undergoes a radical change of consciousness. When this happens the teacher has only to look at the student to recognise that a breakthrough has occurred.

BREAKDOWN, INITIATION AND BRAINWASHING

There are a multitude of ways in which the everyday ego can be broken down: by means of drugs, fatigue, fear, solitude, torture, fasting, meditation, in fact by excessive stimulation or deprivation of any kind (Field 1992). The mechanism of personality breakdown, which is the basis of brainwashing, was first described by the Russian psychologist Pavlov, who discovered it in experimenting on dogs. Given sufficiently prolonged and intense stress his dogs reached the point of breakdown. This could develop into what he called the 'ultra-paradoxical' state where they reversed their former attachments and aversions (Sargant 1959). The technique was used very effectively in the Soviet political trials of the 1930s, and later exploited by repressive forces throughout the world, where political detainees were mentally reprocessed to reject their former convictions and loyalties and love their oppressors.

But from time immemorial reprocessing has also been used constructively in the initiation ceremonies practised by traditional societies. Among the American Indians the transition from boyhood to manhood is mediated by frightening ordeals which lead, via isolation, acute fear and disorientation, to a new level of adult functioning (Brown 1981). The Jewish 'barmitzvah' is a mild, intellectual version of the same process where the young initiate has to present to the elders of his community a portion of the Law. Any situation requiring transition to a new level, whether it involves joining a student society or getting married, is traditionally mediated by initiation ceremonies, and all of them involve the renunciation of the old ego structure and the values attached to it. In its positive aspect it is an aid to growing up, which at the same time involves the loss of innocence. It needs to be remembered that initiation is a form of social processing and imprints on the initiate the values of the particular society he or she has now entered. In this way each society turns out its characteristic products. It then becomes a matter of judgement whether the new values are actually superior to those the initiate formerly subscribed to.

Moreover initiation is frequently abused; this can be seen in the victimisation which occurs to raw army recruits, to new inmates in prison, and new pupils at school. A patient of mine recalled how, in her early months at a girls' boarding school, she was forced to drink her own urine. The breakdown of the ego is obviously a dangerous business and does not always lead to breakthrough. It is therefore important to consider which factors produce a creative or destructive outcome. It would seem that where the process is entered into voluntarily, and where, however harsh the impositions, the initiators seek the welfare of the initiate, the outcome can be a profound development of the personality. But where the pressures are imposed in a destructive spirit, where the purpose is subjugation in order to extract a betrayal or false confession for political purposes, it can result in permanent damage to the personality.

The psychoanalytic equivalent of tribal initiation would be a rigorous analysis where the analysand's 'false self' was thoroughly dismantled so that the true self was enabled to emerge. The function of interpretation itself, in its mutative aspect, is to break down old, maladaptive behavioural responses, so that new ones can take their place. Jung was describing the same process but a different method when he compared therapy to alchemy. The watchword of the spiritual alchemists was '*solve et coagula*' – break down so that you may build up. The alchemists' original aim was to produce gold from the combination of base metals; in psychological terms it means the transformation of base emotions into the true self. In Jungian therapy this takes place in the sealed container of the analytic relationship where changes come about through the intensity of the feelings involved. In psychoanalysis the emphasis is on thought, although in fact intense emotions are generated.

The breaking-down of a patient's defences has also been regarded, sometimes with justification, as a form of brainwashing. Where the analyst lacks a benevolent spirit but is simply doing a job, or where personal commitment is deliberately concealed behind a cold impassivity, breaking down can do much harm and probably accounts for those patients who actually get worse after analytic treatment. In my own practice I have come across several patients who felt convinced that their analyst, over-zealous to liberate them from their narcissism, only succeeded in undermining what little confidence they already had. The analyst might well argue that they were confronting the patient's denial of the truth about themselves. This, of course, rests on the assumption that the analyst always knows the truth and the patient does not. This attitude was conspicuous in Freud's early cases, such as the treatment of Dora and the Wolf Man, where he explicitly took their *denial* of his interpretations as *proof* of their validity:

> We must not be led astray by initial details. If we keep firmly to what we have inferred we shall in the end conquer every resistance by emphasising the unshakeable nature of our convictions.
>
> (Freud 1918)

The danger of the analyst imposing his interpretations on the patient was probably much greater in the early days of psychoanalysis, although it would appear still to prevail among those who maintain an authoritarian style. Thus the French analyst Lacan was known simply to dismiss resistant patients in mid-session. His intention, like that of the Zen master, was perhaps to provoke them into a genuine breakthrough, but his method so scandalised the psychoanalytic establishment that they expelled him.

It is a fact that the almost universal tendency to act submissively towards authority figures is quite alarming; hence the current furore concerning the implantation by counsellors and therapists of 'false memories' of childhood abuse. One legitimate goal of breaking down a patient's resistance is to achieve what Fairbairn called 'the release of bad objects'. In practice this means that where they were mistreated in childhood the patient gives vent to their suppressed rage, instead of pathologically regarding *themselves* as bad in order to preserve their parents as good. This he regarded as central to the therapeutic process; but he also insisted that it can only be applied in a containing and sympathetic context (Fairbairn 1952).

Chapter 3

Healing and exorcism

Just as my training had emphasised the primacy of interpretation, another of its basic tenets was that the proper attitude for the practice of psychotherapy was what Freud termed 'benevolent neutrality'. This was the position I worked hard to sustain in my dealings with patients, but when I reflected more closely on how I actually functioned from session to session it was evident that I deviated from it on numerous occasions. I had to concede that my attitude varied from patient to patient; even within the same session it could shift from the empathic to the confrontational and back again. Just as disturbing was the recognition that with some patients I was often inclined to be challenging while with others it was difficult not to be empathic.

In the empathic mode I listened very closely but said little: it was as if I were engaged in holding the patient within my understanding, as a mother might hold her baby. My interventions felt like a kind of feeding, as if I wished to infuse the patient with a sort of nourishment that would build up their inner strength. Sometimes this connection could deepen into long, comfortable silences that took on an intimate dreaminess. Time itself seemed poised in stillness, as it had with Elaine; and if one of us spoke it seemed not to matter whether or not the other responded. Virtually nothing happened for long periods, yet patients would remember these episodes as confirming, and even creative. Some said it was an experience in which, perhaps for the first time, they felt real. I certainly enjoyed them but later I would feel troubled that, instead of functioning as the alert analyst, I had been simply indulging myself. To allay my guilt I privately hoped my patient might derive some healing from the experience.

In the confrontational mode the climate was decidedly cooler, even bracing. My patient was not held close but was separate, sharply etched in a private otherness. My voice seemed to have acquired an edge and my eye was sharply watchful for every one of the patient's evasions, denials, manipulations and manufactured confusions. Painfully memorable were those sessions where the patient manifestly sabotaged the therapeutic process. At such times I sensed myself in the presence of something stubborn, perverse, destructive; a malign force I felt challenged to expose and defeat. More than once I had the distinct fantasy that I was engaged in a kind of exorcism.

Both these states seemed a long way from the dispassionate objectivity required of the analyst, yet there were occasions when either the nourishing 'healer' or the confronting 'exorcist' proved to be therapeutically effective. Empathic listening certainly relieved agitated patients of their rage or panic; while those I openly challenged might later express their gratitude that I was prepared to do battle with something they had always hated in themselves. I began to reconsider that what I had feared were lapses from orthodox practice might, in fact, have a positive therapeutic effect. The healers and exorcists of earlier ages had been ready to engage deeply with their patients and even to risk their own souls on their behalf. I wondered if a closer look at the work of other contemporary practitioners might reveal that these archaic modes of treatment persisted in our own generation.

THE ROOTS OF PSYCHOTHERAPY

Psychoanalysis was effectively launched with the publication of Freud's and Breuer's *Studies on Hysteria* in 1895. The scientific method itself began with Descartes no more than two hundred years before Freud. But mental illness and its treatment go back to the very beginnings of human society. The activities of the shaman who invoked healing powers with the aid of 'dreams, controlled breathing, repetition' have been described in texts from the Bronze Age (Bromberg 1975). Certain figures on the walls of the caves at Lascaux and Altamira, which reputedly depict the shaman practising his mysterious arts, date back some 15,000 years (Ellenberger 1970). It is in the context of this larger historical perspective that the place and function of modern psychotherapy can usefully be considered.

The history of healing seems to have been an inextricable

mixture of rationality, spirituality, suggestibility, charlatanism, and much else besides. Traditional healing is still actively practised in pre-technological societies all over the world, and even within modern Western society there can be found a wide diversity of alternative healing methods, many of which are associated with neo-religious cults.

While the range of traditional techniques varies enormously, healing derives from a central presupposition about human nature. The medical model treats the body as a physical object that works in the manner of a machine, precisely in accordance with the view of Descartes. Traditional healing makes the radically different assumption that within, besides, or around but certainly prior to the visible body there exists another 'body' that can be neither seen nor touched. This body has been called by many names, such as psyche, soul, or self. The alchemists referred to it as the 'subtle body'; it is 'mana' among the Melanesians, 'wakonda' amongst the American Indians, 'ch'i' amongst the Chinese, 'prana' on the Indian subcontinent. In modern times Bergson called it 'élan vital', Groddeck the 'It', Freud the 'id', Jung 'the collective unconscious', Reich 'orgone energy'; and more recently, Mindell devised the intriguing name 'dreambody'. It is doubtful if there exists a language that does not make reference to it.

It has always been regarded as incorporating both the natural and supernatural, and the shaman, as one who could enter the supernatural domain, has been accorded a special status as both healer and priest. The shaman's principal function was the retrieval of lost souls. According to ancient belief the soul may be stolen by an evil spirit, especially during sleep. It is the shaman's job to track it down, bargain, or do battle, with its captors, and return it safely to its owner. There is abundant documentation of shamanic healing from every part of the globe. Specific procedures vary from tribe to tribe and continent to continent, but in all of them the shaman does his or her work by entering into a trance. Eliade describes a characteristic practice among the tribes of Siberia:

> the Tremyugan shaman begins beating his drum and playing the guitar until he falls into an ecstasy. Abandoning his body his soul enters the underworld and goes in search of the patient's soul. He persuades the dead to let him bring it back to earth by promising them the gift of a shirt or other thing; sometimes he is

obliged to use more forcible means. When he wakes from his ecstasy the shaman has the patient's soul in his closed hand and replaces it in the body through the right ear.

(Eliade 1964: 220)

All this seems a far cry from the analyst in an armchair: how can he or she remotely be compared to a healer in a trance? First we must ask if there exists a modern equivalent to the condition known as 'loss of soul'. In his description of the schizoid personality, Fairbairn offers the following profile: 'the individual begins to tell us that he feels as if there were nothing of him, or as if he had lost his identity, or as if he were dead, or as if he had ceased to exist' (Fairbairn 1952).

If this state deteriorates still further we reach the schizophrenic conditions of depersonalisation and derealisation which Fairbairn termed the 'ultimate psychological disaster' of 'loss of ego' (1952: 3). If we take 'loss of ego' to be the equivalent of the age-old notion of 'loss of soul' then psychoanalytic theory comes very close to the basic presupposition of shamanic healing. I referred earlier to Ferenczi's relaxation technique which, like hypnotism, had the effect of putting patients into trance-like states. Jung came nearer to the function of the shaman in that, according to his method, it was not the patient who went into trance but the analyst. Jung advocated that the therapist induce or allow in him- or herself what he called 'a lowering of consciousness' (1954: 180–1). In this state the conscious faculties can be allowed to fall temporarily into abeyance producing, in my own experience, a dreamy state where the centre of energy and connectedness is felt to be located not so much in the head but somewhere around the solar plexus. Similar twentieth-century accounts can be found in Balint who speaks of a 'harmonious, interpenetrating mix-up' (1958: 66) and in Searles who calls it 'pre-ambivalent symbiosis' (1965: 536–43). These are only two practitioners among a host of others who report entering into states of fusion with their patient, so that it became impossible to determine where one ended and the other began. Here is a vivid example of this type of interaction by the Jungian analyst Schwartz-Salant:

At this point something unusual happened. As I was aware of the incestuous link she had with her brother, I experienced an erotic energy field between us. She also experienced it. As we both felt this energy, which seemed like something between us, my consciousness lowered a bit and, just as in active imagination, I saw a shimmering image, which partook of both of us, move upwards from where it was, near the ground. I told her this. She said: 'Yes, I also see it, but I'm afraid of it.' I continued to share what I saw and experienced. I saw the image between us as white; she saw a kind of fluid that had a centre. She said she knew if she descended into her body it would be too intense, that she was afraid. She stated that she felt I was now her friend, that it felt like a I–Thou relationship, and that she had never before had such a relationship with anyone. . . . A feeling of timelessness pervaded; I didn't know if one minute or twenty had passed. . . . She said she felt I was extremely powerful and sensual, but for the first time this didn't frighten her because she felt equality. A sense of kinship, a brother–sister feeling, was clear to both of us. And there was a pull towards sexual enactment, towards physical union, but this tendency had its own inhibition, as if the energy field between us oscillated, separating and joining us in a kind of sine wave rhythm . . . it resulted in a remarkable transformation of Mary's inner life.

(Schwartz-Salant 1984: 16)

In my own experience the lowering of consciousness has sometimes been actually very difficult to fight against. In working with my patient Noreen I had a marked reluctance to engage with her. This was due to the fact that she spontaneously aroused in me, from the moment she entered the room, a feeling of cold indifference amounting to contempt. There was no rational reason why I should feel this way, especially as I knew Noreen to be a lonely and unhappy woman. My negativity was so marked, and so consistent, that I had no doubt that I had introjected the hatred Noreen entertained towards herself. I knew myself to be 'possessed' by a sadistic countertransference, but in spite of this awareness every session began with my trying to overcome my stultifying boredom with everything she said. We would engage in what sounded like a serious analytic dialogue, but every discussion always grew increasingly hollow and petered out. One important topic was the possibility that her deep self-hatred was connected with a psychologically incestuous relationship with her father. It seemed to me that they had been close to an unwholesome degree, presumably to the exclusion of her mother, which had left Noreen with very bad feelings. But no amount of insightful exchange between us could change this cold, lifeless relationship that imposed itself at every session.

At the same time I would be fighting off an increasingly oppressive sense of drowsiness, as if I was being forcibly anaesthetised. It was a singularly horrible experience, since my drowsiness was pervaded by a sense of utter bleakness and depletion. So drained and chilled did I feel that even on the warmest summer day I wanted to switch on the electric fire. Sometimes I speculated that this was how it might feel to be dying of hypothermia or loss of blood. At other times I felt that an immense force was pressing on my chest, drilling through me, and evoked the fantasy of being 'bored to death'.

Sleepiness would eventually overwhelm me, and in the face of it, Noreen would fall silent. After months of this unhappy routine she gave up, but not by ending the therapy (which she would most certainly have been justified in doing) but by closing her eyes and dropping off to sleep herself. We dozed for about ten minutes. Mine was not a normal sleep, but drugged, full of intense dream fragments. With about a third of the session remaining we would awaken, rather sheepishly, and resume our dialogue. But by now a remarkable change had taken place. My sadistic indifference had changed into normal empathy: Noreen had been restored into someone who mattered. She herself often said that, for the first time that week, she felt 'normal'; and we would now engage in what felt a fruitful, even creative, discussion. I speculated that the shift in me from hostile indifference to a decent human connection reflected a shift within Noreen from self-loathing to self-acceptance. Somehow, in sleep, the devils had been banished or transformed, and we could now talk like two human beings.

The sleep phase imposed itself at every session, as if it were a power I was helpless to resist. This proved to be not just my fantasy, because when we discussed it, Noreen confessed to a curious feeling that she was somehow hypnotising me. But after two years of this tormenting routine I decided I could take no more and initiated an ending of the therapy. Noreen reluctantly agreed, although we had not quite achieved a sense of completion. I said goodbye to her with much relief, but at the same time feeling guilty that I was abandoning her. About a year later she wrote to tell me of a memory which she thought might account for the bad feelings she had towards herself. She said that a childhood recollection had suddenly come to her, with near-hallucinatory intensity, of sitting on her father's lap while he masturbated. She was now certain that the abuse had been more than psychological. Although the therapy had failed to uncover this crucial memory she said she was very grateful for our work together, and most especially 'for the sleeps' which she felt had somehow restored her sense of self. How this was accomplished I am not sure. It may be that the shared intimacy of 'sleeping together' provided a mother–baby connection deficient in Noreen's infancy; or perhaps a father–daughter intimacy but without abuse. An additional possibility is that, by putting me into a trance, she recreated the conditions of healing whereby some vital, unconscious contact was repeatedly made between us which slowly neutralised her deathly alienation.

POSSESSION

But healing alone may be insufficient to meet the challenge that mental disturbance presents. In a great many patients it seems as if, in addition to the urge to become well, there is some obstinate counter force that acts as a saboteur, an alien presence that actively resists the therapy and which, with each increase in wellbeing, seems to fight back ever more viciously.

As well as 'loss of soul', the principal mental disorder that primitive man suffered was the state known as 'possession'. In the classical cases the victim was thought to have been invaded by a spirit, usually that of a dead parent. Often the possessed individual remained aware of his individual self but 'feels a spirit within his own spirit'. In other cases there is a total loss of identity. The features change and take on a striking resemblance to the possessor; voice and speech likewise correspond with uncanny similitude (Ellenberger 1970: 13).

The ancient method of countering possession was exorcism, known to have been practised for many thousands of years by peoples of the Mediterranean basin: Jews, Muslims and Christians. The exorcist's first task was to compel the spirit to say his name. Once this was known, the exorcist would forcibly command the spirit to depart. A vivid description may be found in Aldous Huxley's account of an exorcism by a Fr. Barré in 1632 of Sister Jeanne, prioress of the convent at Loudun:

speaking through the lips of the demoniac, Asmodeus revealed he was entrenched in the lower belly. For more than two hours Barre wrestled with him: 'I exorcise thee, most unclean spirit, every onslaught of the Adversary, every spectre, every legion, in the name of our Lord, Jesus Christ: be thou uprooted and put to flight from this creature of God.' And then there would be a sprinkling of holy water, a laying on of hands, a laying on of the stole, of the breviary, of relics. 'I abjure thee, ancient serpent, by the judge of the living and the dead, by thy maker, by the maker of the world, by him who has the power to cast thee into Gehenna, that from this servant of God, who hastens back to the bosom of the Church, thou with the fears and afflictions of thy fury, speedily depart.'

(Huxley 1952: 113)

Fairbairn describes the contemporary psychotherapist as 'the true successor to the exorcist...he is concerned not only with the "forgiveness of sins" but with the "casting out of devils" ' (Fairbairn 1952: 70). But we may well ask: what are these devils and how did they get there in the first place? If we look more closely at psychoanalytic theory we should be able to identify what might be regarded as two kinds of devils.

'Cases of demoniacal possession,' wrote Freud (1923b: 436–72) 'correspond to the neuroses of the present day. What in those days were thought to be evil spirits to us are base and evil wishes, the derivatives of impulses which have been rejected and repressed.' These could be called instinctual devils, part of our natural but socially tabooed inheritance. But, in addition, there are also introjected devils, or what psychoanalysis calls 'internalised bad objects'. It is now well understood, thanks to object relations theory, that the internalisation of important figures of our childhood is a major dynamic of personality development. Whether for good or ill, it could be said that we are all 'possessed'. Fairbairn took the view that it is a universal human characteristic to defensively introject an unsatisfactory, even damaging, parental figure rather than to have no parent at all. Thus an abused child almost inevitably introjects the abusing adult and frequently becomes an abuser in later life – becomes, in a sense, possessed by a devil.

Meltzer echoes the medieval categories of demonology by connecting psychopathology with zones inside the 'internalised mother'. Thus in the above quotation from Huxley the demon Asmodeus was described as located in the 'lower belly', or what Meltzer (1992) called the 'claustrum'. This offers 'the pleasures of sadism, masochism, power, wiliness, deception' – all familiar pastimes of hell.

A vivid example of 'introjection-possession' emerged while I was working with a married couple. Once the wife had completed a critical catalogue of her husband's shortcomings, he proceeded to defend himself in a low, angry monotone. I noticed that his voice sounded different from normal, the words seeming to issue from somewhere inside him while his mouth hardly moved. When I eventually commented on the eerie effect this produced his wife triumphantly declared: 'Now you've heard it – that's his father – it's his father's voice.' The husband agreed that his father, who had been a missionary, spoke in the same liturgical monotone both when he preached and when he admonished his son. Under pressure, the son reproduced precisely the tone and style of his father's voice 'like a man possessed'.

The addiction to a bad object is a serious problem in psychotherapeutic treatment. It is as if a spirit of negativity pits itself against the life force that the therapy tries to mobilise. With his usual clinical acumen Freud observed it in his patients and labelled it the 'negative therapeutic reaction'. I can recall one instance in which a patient, with what felt uncannily like diabolical obstinacy, literally retorted: 'Say what you like, I *will not yield to you.*' In the face of such perverse resistance a benign 'healing' attitude is quite ineffectual. The therapist who submits to it only provokes the patient to denigrate him or her still further, thereby becoming the victim of the patient's own internalised abuser. In these situations the confrontational style of psychoanalysis, with its readiness to challenge and unmask, is essential, and this is the modern equivalent of exposing and driving out the demons.

In practice, confrontation means taking on the patient's anger and not being intimidated by it. Searles observes:

> the relationship between patient and therapist must gradually grow... strong enough for the therapist to endure the fullest intensity of the patient's hostility... and, complementarily, I have found it an equally essential part of this phase that the therapist finds himself gradually coming, step by step, to

express openly – even though not as often as he feels it – the very fullest intensity of his own hatred, condemnation, and contempt towards the patient.

(Searles 1965)

I would qualify this statement in one vital particular: that the hatred should be directed not at the patient but at the 'demon' that possesses him. In practice it is far from easy for those in the helping professions to express hatred towards a patient, even when it is 'objective hatred' as Winnicott recommends. Here is one example:

> In his third year, he suddenly ground to a halt, and fell violently silent, exuding ever stronger black waves of hatred and despair. . . . His gaze, when he glanced at me, was shifty, evil, and terrified. He was as if possessed. . . . I carried dark and heavy projective identifications, to put it one way, which I tried in vain to decode to him, until I was almost as saturated in despair as he was. One day, without thinking it out clearly. . . I simply and suddenly became furious for his prolonged lethal attack on me and on the analysis. I wasn't going to stand it a moment longer, I shouted, without the remotest idea at that moment of what alternative I was proposing. This outburst of mine changed the course of the analysis.

(Coltart 1986)

Coltart remarks that her patient 'was as if possessed': I suggest that he really was possessed by a malevolent internal object which she spontaneously exorcised.

Among the depth psychologists of the twentieth century many bear the imprint of healers: Jung, Ferenczi, Winnicott, Milner, Balint, to name only some of the most eminent. They appear to have a trust in some pre-existing healing power in both themselves and their patients and a readiness to find ways whereby it can become mobilised. By contrast Melanie Klein and her school sound more like exorcists. They readily 'name the devils', actively confront denial, resistance, manipulation, seduction, exposing all the carefully hidden manifestations of negative transference, disguised sadism, and a hatred of the truth that analysis seeks to uncover. Hence patients in Kleinian analysis are inclined to remark: 'It's awful, my analyst is giving me a very bad time, but I do feel I'm getting somewhere.'

Confrontation meets a deep inner need for self-cleansing, a

stripping away of flabby excrescence. It is an expression of the urge to break down the old maladapted ego in order to make a new beginning. In an earlier, less materialistic, culture it expressed itself in an ascetic style of life, taken to an extreme by the austerities of the Desert Fathers. In its secular form it becomes an obsessive type of perfectionism, masochistic and self-hating: in women it is often somatised as anorexia; in men by engaging in dangerous or brutal sports, surviving hardship, or travelling to inhospitable places in order to find themselves.

The victim of childhood abuse who becomes, in turn, an abuser has taken in an alien introject that requires to be named, confronted and expelled. But there are an equal number of instances where a patient has split off and become unconsciously dominated by a part of his or her own instinctual personality – be it anger, envy, rivalry – and this calls not for expulsion but reintegration. Here the appropriate response is healing. Namely the infantile characteristic must first be recognised and accepted; and thereafter the natural developmental process can get to work and render it not simply harmless but a dynamic part of the total personality.

Healing and exorcism are usually regarded as distinct modes of treatment: thus the healing attitude is strongly inclined towards empathy, genuineness, warmth and confirmation. In accounts of exorcism we enter a harsher climate: one of command, emotional violence, danger and intensity. But it would be simplistic to see them as mutually exclusive. Traditionally the exorcist, even as he or she drives out the demons, prays for the patient's soul; the healer not only recovers lost souls, he or she readily does battle with the evil spirits that have captured it. The difficulty for the psychotherapist is to manage both.

Chapter 4

Mechanisms and mysteries

Yvonne was one of my earliest cases and a failure, in that she came for just a few sessions and then left. It was an encounter that, although brief, left me deeply disturbed. She was a young woman in her middle twenties, the daughter of a doctor. Even in our first session it became evident how intensely attached she was to her father, although they seemed to be constantly quarrelling. She was even more preoccupied with a young man with whom she said she was in love. She felt he was growing indifferent to her and she spoke quite obsessively about her fear of losing him.

I listened carefully and tried hard to make sense of her intense anxiety. But after just three or four visits the problems with both father and lover became overshadowed by a new complication. She reported that as she had approached my consulting room that day she had suddenly felt dizzy. I was puzzled and did not take it up. We moved on to the topic of her increasing jealousy for a young woman whom she suspected was becoming interested in her lover. At her next visit she told me she had felt quite ill on nearing my house and had thought of turning back. I began to feel uneasy. Two sessions later she reported that, as she rang my bell, her legs suddenly folded under her, and had she not hung onto the railings she would have sunk to the ground. By now I was quite alarmed. Instead of deriving benefit from her sessions Yvonne was growing ever more disturbed. My training had not prepared me for whatever was happening and my supervisor was still on holiday.

I brooded anxiously on this complication: why did she keep collapsing? Her symptoms spoke plainly of a powerful instinctive aversion to coming to see me. Why should that be? Had my interpretations disclosed aspects of her personality she dreaded to face? It hardly seemed possible; I still understood so little about her, I had so far made only the most tentative of comments. Or was there something damaging about me which her unconscious was reacting against? Her faintness and falling were clearly hysterical, which suggested some sexual complication. But that could hardly involve me; I was almost old enough to be her father. Besides, she was desperate about losing her lover.

In the following session something even more disturbing occurred. She was again telling me about her jealousy for her rival. I asked if, when she was younger, she could remember having been jealous of her mother? Her response was to burst into tears. I was astonished at her reaction – but even more at my own! At the sight of her heaving abandoned sobs I felt a sudden surge of sexual excitement. As I realised what was happening to me I felt quite appalled. This young woman was my patient: how could I have such a bizarre reaction? I frantically wondered if I had been harbouring repressed sexual desires towards her. If so, they were quite remote from consciousness; nor did I find her particularly attractive. Barely able to concentrate, I got through the session as best I could. As her tears subsided so did my arousal. When the session ended I was profoundly shaken, but thankful that she had no suspicion of her effect on me.

She came only a few more times. Her fainting symptoms seemed to get worse and she decided to stop. My relief was marginally greater than my disappointment at losing a patient after so few sessions. When my supervisor returned from holiday we began to work out why Yvonne had developed such a resistance to coming. In the supervisor's view the fact that I was about the same age as her father, so far from disqualifying me, made me all too suitable as the object of passionate feelings she had entertained for her father in childhood. This had created such an unconscious conflict about forbidden desires that her whole body prevented her from crossing my threshold. My supervisor noted that what had re-emerged in the therapeutic setting was the familiar Oedipal transference. Familiar it might have been, but encountered in this way it struck me as nonetheless remarkable. How could this somewhat hysterical but essentially sane young woman harbour the illusion that I was the father she had known and loved from childhood onwards?

THE RIDDLE OF TRANSFERENCE

Over the years I have come to realise that the therapeutic setting may look ordinary enough – just two people talking in a room – but in fact it can evoke extraordinary reactions. The consulting room is a space sealed off from the everyday world and what happens there can be quite different from everyday life. As the patient you are given the freedom to say whatever comes to mind, no matter how bizarre, compromising or offensive. You know that whatever you express is confidential, with the implicit promise it will be heard without approval or criticism. But over against this unprecedented freedom there is an equal measure of restriction. You may talk but must not act. You must come and go only at the agreed times, and pay for the privilege. You disclose your most private thoughts and fantasies to a stranger who tells you nothing about himself. Although you know nothing about the analyst, in some mysterious way he or she becomes the most intimate of strangers.

I suggest that this combination of freedom and restriction, of closeness and distance, has a profound effect. The requirement to give one's thoughts and feelings free reign yet at the same time to observe them happening creates a subtle dislocation in the mind and, together with all the other factors activates regression, whereupon the illusions of transference begin to manifest. In Yvonne's case the child that was still so alive in her rapidly came to experience me as her father. Had her regression gone even deeper, she may well have experienced me as her mother; or both parents combined. It is as if the therapist and patient function as a one-parent family. Or perhaps not even a parent but a part of one, a pair of arms, or a lap to sit on; even just a voice, a smell, a presence that transforms cold into warmth, isolation into life. Through regression we enter a different dimension of experience.

Although the analytic setting has a particular power to produce these illusions, they constantly happen in everyday life. We frequently project onto all kinds of people – teachers, doctors, policemen – qualities we once attributed to the significant figures of our childhood. Like transitional objects they are both found and created. There are in everyday life a great many other illusion-making situations besides therapy, one of the most familiar being a film show. As in the therapy session, the world goes about its business outside the cinema, but for a little while the illusions of the screen take precedence. What we watch are not merely shadows on a screen but something more 'real' than the muted roar of the traffic rumbling by outside. On a theatre stage a room may be presented to look like an ordinary suburban lounge, but since one side is open to the audience that too is an illusion, a space set aside from real life. But it is more than an illusion; it is a place where the events transacted take on a special degree of meaning.

The point I am making is that in the midst of our everyday existence we set aside spaces for the actualisation of another kind of reality, and the therapy situation happens to be one of them. What happens in the therapeutic space happens, so to speak, in a different dimension from the everyday world, and obliges us to realise that reality manifests not only at the familiar level of waking consciousness but operates in several other dimensions as well, each carrying its own validity. This has a crucial bearing on our understanding of consciousness in general and on psychotherapy in particular.

THE RIDDLE OF EMBODIED COUNTER-TRANSFERENCE

Although I discussed my patient's symptoms with my supervisor, I never had the courage to discuss my own. It was not simply that it was too embarrassing. I really feared she might consider me psychologically abnormal, or morally unfit to continue my training. So I was left to puzzle out my bizarre reaction for myself. With longer experience I discovered that I was prone to other types of spontaneous bodily reactions. As already indicated, I could rapidly be overcome by acute drowsiness, or could find myself afflicted at a certain point in the session by violent trembling. Sometimes it gripped me even as the patient entered the room. Nothing like this had ever happened to me before I began to practice. The odd thing was that I could be sexually aroused regardless of whether or not I found my patient attractive; or I would tremble with fear in the presence of a seemingly inoffensive patient half my size; or become almost anaesthetised while listening to a lively or urgent story.

The phenomenon was so intrusive and so baffling that I would nervously enquire of colleagues if they had experienced anything similar. The majority knew nothing of such symptoms; some suggested I needed more analysis or better supervision; others said if I kept getting drowsy perhaps I was simply overtired. I knew this to be untrue in that I would wake from my sleepiness in mid-session, or with the arrival of the next patient. Quite a few therapists admitted suffering from overwhelming sleepiness, fewer to sexual arousal. There were others who admitted that with certain patients they would have inexplicable surges of physical hunger, stabbing pains in the body, tears, a sudden sensitivity to noises in the street; sometimes even the ticking of the clock became deafening. It was a relief not to feel too abnormal.

In time I became increasingly convinced that these somatic innervations were a way of picking up messages from the patient's unconscious. And this recognition began to explain what had happened with Yvonne. Freud's Oedipus theory made explicit the fact that there exists between parents and their children a powerful erotic bond. Forced into repression by the incest taboo, it often takes the form of a father's excessive control of his daughter's behaviour and interests. Legitimised in the name of parental protection, it is really an expression of possessive jealousy and can result in passionate quarrelling. From what Yvonne had told me she and her father were certainly entangled in this sado-maso-chistic way. It would seem that, given my role as her therapist, I was rapidly installed in my patient's unconscious as a father figure, so that her repressed attraction for her real father was superimposed on her sessions with me. Hence her unconscious resistance to coming to see me. She heard my question concerning her jealousy of her mother as an exposure of her shameful feelings, and burst into tears. But they were not only tears of shame; they were an admission of her forbidden desires. I reacted to them as if I had received an erotic declaration, which produced in me an involuntary erotic response. But it was more than a response; it was as if her repressed desire (or, through identification, her father's desire) went directly into my unconscious and I assumed it was my own.

What I had experienced in this directly physical way is an example of the now familiar phenomenon of countertransference, where the patient succeeds in inducing feelings of all kinds in the analyst – indifference, elation, blankness, hopelessness, warmth, etc. Equally the analyst may find him or herself having dreams or fantasies that refer to the patient, either directly or symbolically. Or it may affect the analyst's behaviour, so that the analyst finds him or herself subtly indulging or punishing the patient. In whatever form it manifests, it means the patient has 'got under his skin', as Balint noted (1958: 18). How can such reactions come about? The analyst Roger Money-Kyrle (1956: 366), in discussing the phenomenon of countertransference, comments: 'How exactly a patient does succeed in imposing a phantasy and its corresponding affect upon his analyst is a most interesting problem.' He offers a common-sense scientific explanation:

> I do not think we need assume some form of extra-sensory communication; but the communication can be of a pre-verbal and archaic kind – similar perhaps to that used by gregarious animals in which a posture or call of a single member will arouse a corresponding affect in the rest.
>
> (Money-Kyrle 1956)

However Money-Kyrle seems not entirely satisfied by his own speculations, since he continues:

> In the analytic situation a peculiarity of this kind is that, at first sight, they do not seem as if they had been made by the patient at all. The analyst experiences the affect as being his own response to something.
>
> (Money-Kyrle 1956)

Between Yvonne and myself an explicit communication did pass: her explosion of tears. But my response was to quite a different message. How did I contrive to receive it? The phenomenon that Money-Kyrle refers to was originally noted by Jung and called 'psychic infection' or 'participation mystique'. It was later observed independently by Melanie Klein and elaborated into her theory of projective identification; she offered a persuasive explanation in terms of phantasised attacks by an infant on its mother:

> [It] derives from anal and urethral impulses and implies expelling dangerous substances [excrements] out of the self into the mother. . . . In so far as the mother comes to contain bad parts of the self, she is not felt to be a separate individual but is felt to be the bad self.
>   Much of the hatred against parts of the self is now directed against the mother. This leads to a particular form of aggression

which establishes the prototype of an aggressive object relation. I suggest for this process the term projective identification.

(Klein 1946: 8)

What Klein had noted in its aggressive aspect was further explored by other analysts, notably W.R. Bion, and the process of projective identification came to be recognised as a universal factor in human development. Whether it occurs between a mother and her baby, analyst and patient, or any two or more people, it proceeds in three stages:

First there is the fantasy of projecting a part of oneself into another person and of that part taking over the person from within; then there is a pressure exerted via the interpersonal interaction such that the 'recipient' of the projection experiences pressure to think, feel, and behave in a manner congruent with the projection; finally the projected feelings, after having been 'psychologically processed' by the recipient, are re-internalised by the projector.

(Ogden 1979: 358)

In this account the recipient is used in the manner of a dialysis machine which takes in the donor's 'poison', detoxifies it, and passes it back. Other analysts, such as Searles, have noted that good feelings suffer the same fate: they get split off and lodged in the recipient who then feels unjustifiably good about himself. It is the basis of the hysterical love relationship, where one party adores the other who cheerfully basks in his (or her) new-found, albeit ill-founded, wellbeing. It happens routinely in the therapeutic situation where the patient projects his or her own omnipotence onto the analyst who is endowed with magical healing powers. It is the therapist's task not to bask in these gratifying feelings but to process them, so that the donor can eventually re-internalise them in a more realistic form.

Although the account given by the mechanism of projective identification is enormously helpful, it still leaves a number of questions unanswered. How is it possible that a bit of one person's psyche can lodge itself in the psyche of another? How does that bit jump across the intervening space? How did I, for example, acquire the immediate conviction that the sexual arousal was entirely my own, rather like a deluded bird into whose nest a cuckoo's egg had been deposited?

In my embarrassing encounter with Yvonne I had come up against the mystery of unconscious communication. Freud had long before noted: 'It is a very remarkable thing that the unconscious of one human being can react upon another, without passing through consciousness' (Freud 1915: 126). In an attempt to elucidate this mystery he had written several papers on what he called 'thought transference'. He admitted that he was very tempted to explore this area further but decided to direct his mind to other manifestations of the unconscious, such as dreams, slips of the tongue, etc., thereby laying the foundation of psychoanalysis.

ANALYSIS AND THE PARANORMAL

I think we must recognise that projective and introjective identification, especially in its embodied form, has all the characteristics of a paranormal phenomenon. The fact that it occurs routinely in the therapeutic situation does not make it any less extraordinary. In so far as classical analysis has always striven to achieve the objectivity of classical science, it is not surprising that Freud's work on thought transference, in which he was much influenced by Ferenczi, was hardly followed up. However, several analysts of a later generation – Servadio and Ehrenwald, among others – noted that the dreams of certain of their patients could, on occasion, show a baffling familiarity with their private affairs although they had never disclosed anything of their personal lives. Some, like Istvan Hollos (1953), speculated that 'thought transference' had as much to do with the analyst as the patient, and hypothesised an unconscious interplay between them. Jung had a fascination for the paranormal from early in his career, but this did little to enhance his credibility with the analytic establishment, and it remains a dubious area.

In the 1970s a group of Jungian analysts in Berlin set up a research project to investigate the unconscious interaction between analyst and patient. It ran for a period of over two years. I quote their conclusions:

> During this period the most astonishing fact was a complete correspondence between the analyst's and the patient's chain of associations ... [in addition there was] an astonishing increase in the phenomena of synchronicity, especially in sessions with

archetypal dreams and of high emotional stress . . . as we started
to keep more accurate records of the subliminal perceptions of
the analyst so the incidence of these events (synchronicity and
ESP) increased.

(Diekmann 1976).

From a rational viewpoint it is difficult to understand how
messages can be transmitted outside of our five senses. Investiga-
tions into paranormal phenomena usually enlist the notion of
psychic energy, notably Rhine's PK effect, as the medium of
communication. But to the present day psychic energy has not
been known to register on any scientific instrument, much to the
frustration of psychic research. I wish to offer an alternative
explanation: it may be that we have to grapple with the mystery
of how a thought, feeling, fantasy, even an entire personality, can
be projected from one psyche into another because we are
operating with an inadequate model of the mind. Most analytic
discussion of projective identification explores solely the unconscious of the patient. But we are faced with the whole problem of
transmission only because we assume that the parties involved are
separate entities to begin with. But if, at some unconscious level,
they are already merged no transfer is required, since in a state of
merger what happens to one happens to the other.

Given the fact that each of us feels ourself to be, and looks to
others to be, a separate individual, the notion that we also exist in a
state of merger puts a heavy strain on our credulity. We can allow
the poet licence to declare that 'no man is an island', but to accept it
as a literal truth is a different matter. But this, in fact, was Jung's
position. He compared individual consciousness to islands standing up in the sea; if we look below the surface we realise that at the
level of the sea bed we are joined. Somehow we have to entertain
the paradoxical notion that, as living beings, we are both separate
and united. From the viewpoint of everyday consciousness we
appear to be separate individuals with a regrettable tendency to
relapse into fantasies of fusion; but if we could look through the
other end of the telescope it could be argued that the fact of our
connection is the primary reality and our separateness a secondary one. This is not to denigrate human individuality but to
emphasise how fragile it is, and how vigilantly we must protect it.

If there does exist, as Jung proposed, a more fundamental,
collective unconscious, we could ask: is it restricted only to the

human species, or could we envisage some vast sea of consciousness which we share with *all* living creatures? Or beyond that, with an infinite continuum that underlies existence itself? Having set out to investigate the riddles posed by phenomena such as transference and projective identification, we are led to what must seem blatantly unscientific speculations. Yet serious support for such ideas has been coming from science itself for many years – from contemporary research in physics, mathematics, astronomy, and the major life sciences. The gathering evidence, for example in mind and brain research, has developed into a field of study that is expanding with unprecedented rapidity. The profound implications for the future of psychotherapy justifies my offering a brief restatement, enriched by an abundance of quotations from leading workers in the field, of what are now widely accepted ideas.

Chapter 5

New science and old philosophies

Throughout history every system of belief has subscribed to a cosmology in which spirit created matter, commonly acknowledged in the phrase that 'in the beginning God made heaven and earth'. This universal assumption, unquestioned for millennia, began to change in the seventeenth century with the evolution of the scientific method. This involved the basic assumptions that every event is produced by an antecedent cause, that the greater is explained by the smaller, and that what is mental and spiritual is derived from the material.

When Copernicus mathematically proved that the world was not a huge stationary disc occupying the entire firmament but a relatively minute sphere rotating in a very large universe, science and religion became increasingly open enemies. This shift from a two- to a three-dimensional image of the world – that it was a sphere and not a disc – brought momentous consequences. The assurance that you could not fall off the earth's edge led to the European discovery of the Americas. The development of the scientific method led to the wholesale industrialisation of society, which in turn transformed every aspect of the existing culture. In Western society this involved the general decline of religious belief, and with it the increasing dominance of a materialistic view of existence.

Just three centuries later an even greater scientific revolution has taken place, this time from a three- to a four-dimensional model of the universe. In the early years of this century microphysics found itself confronting a sub-atomic world where 'particles are both destructible and non-destructible, matter is both continuous and discontinuous, and force and matter are but different aspects of the same phenomenon' (Capra 1970: 152).

In order to make sense of such paradoxical phenomena Einstein was obliged to transcend the three-dimensional logic of Newtonian physics for a four-dimensional space–time, which is the basis of his Special Theory of Relativity. We habitually conceive of space as three-dimensional, and time (which appears to flow from the future back into the past) as one-dimensional. In everyday experience space and time are manifestly different, but Einstein's theory of relativity joins them together.

By the 1920s the findings of quantum mechanics had become firmly established. In 1929 Pauli and Heisenberg jointly presented their field theory that matter and energy are manifestations of another level of reality, the level of the quantum fields. It had been verified experimentally that the law of cause and effect holds good down to the level of the molecule, but in the sub-atomic world events become less predictable; matter ceases to be solid stuff but comprises minutely elusive electrical impulses in a changing network of relationships. These are not networks of particles, but networks per se. Particles can only be said to exist if they are observed. Grasping an idea like this is like watching the Cheshire Cat disappear while only the grin remains. According to Heisenberg's Uncertainty Principle the realm of the quantum is ruled by sheer probability. In more precise terms the more the observer knows of the mass of a particle the less can be known of its velocity. The choice of observing one aspect of nature involves the sacrifice of the other. Something similar happens in everyday life: by making an experience conscious we unavoidably sacrifice something of its immediacy.

Throughout the twentieth century scientific discovery moved away from the old iron law of prediction and objectivity and towards indeterminacy and subjectivity. Bell's theorem, published in 1964, and based on experiments by Einstein, Podolsky and Rosen, mathematically proved the extraordinary phenomenon that when two sub-atomic particles have once interacted any interference with one particle will instantaneously affect the other, regardless of the distance between them. This reveals what Bohm called 'the quantum interconnectedness of distant systems' and 'proves that the ordinary idea of an objective world unaffected by consciousness lies in opposition not only to quantum theory but to facts established by experiment' (Dossey 1985: 132).

Quantum mechanics seriously weakens the basic assumption of Newtonian physics that nature exists as an objective reality, that there exists an external world quite unconnected to our internal one. The physicist John Wheeler commented on this elemental change: 'To describe what has happened one has to cross out the word "observer" and put in its place the new word "participator". In some strange sense the universe is a participatory universe' (quoted in Dossey 1985: 195).

A further unravelling of the certainties of classical science came about with the invention of holography. One fascination of the hologram is that any bit of it will reproduce not just that particular segment but the entire image, albeit in a more diffuse version. The paradox of the whole being contained in the part has prompted several very radical theories. The neuroscientist Karl Pribram has argued that the human brain itself functions holographically (Pribram 1982: 27–34): it constructs our reality by interpreting frequencies from another 'domain' that, like Einstein's fourth dimension, transcends time and space.

The physicist David Bohm extended the holographic concept to incorporate our perception of the universe itself: that what we see 'out there' is identical to our brain processes 'in here'; that what we are looking *at* is what we are looking *with* (Bohm 1982: 46). Bohm, a distinguished colleague of Einstein, regarded the so-called objective universe as a mental construct, which he called the explicate order. In essence it is an illusion, a lesser order of reality, and underlying it is the implicate order from which it emanates. In Bohm's terms, every bit of the explicate order must be a holographic fragment of the implicate order and carries its original imprint.

In making assertions of this kind we have moved from physics to metaphysics, and are confronted with the fundamental question: what is real? Common sense tells us that the real is what we can touch, see, hear, smell and taste. Yet dreams produce all these sense data, and we know, from subjective experience, that dreams belong to a different order from the reality of waking life. How real is my sense of myself? How real are Freud's ego, id, superego, Jung's complexes and archetypes? Are they simply operational concepts that enable us to think? Is a thought or feeling real? Pain certainly feels very real, whether the doctor can find the cause for it or not. Neither a pain nor a dream can be inspected on a laboratory bench; at best their presence can be inferred by measuring varying levels of electrical activity in the brain. And this is precisely the evidence provided by the fundamental constituents of matter itself – the quarks, mesons, and sub-atomic particles which show up as streaks and points of light on the researcher's television screen.

Where Pribram applied holographic theory to explain certain baffling aspects of brain function such as memory, modern biochemistry focuses on the recent discovery of the neuro-transmitters in the blood stream which regulate bodily health in the most subtle and intricate ways. These minute cells, which are activated by every passing thought and feeling, seem to lie on the borderline between mind and body. A detailed description of their function is provided by the endocrinologist Deepak Chopra (1989). His main argument is very similar to that of Pribram, namely that the physical body would appear to be the embodi-ment of a mysterious intelligence whose roots lie in the 'quan-tum' zone.

The Jungian analyst David Tresan has researched extensively at the interface of psychotherapy and neuroscience and is especially interested in the fundamental shift of outlook that has taken place in the area of mind–brain studies. One senior neuroscientist, Walter Freeman, is quoted by Tresan as saying:

> There is no question that some shift of immense magnitude is taking place in our understanding of ourselves, but none of us has the perspective yet to grasp its nature and significance.
>
> (Tresan 1996)

But some things are now generally agreed: that reductionism no longer furnishes an adequate explanation of all phenomena, least of all those involving living forms and mental activity. This shift has loosened the stranglehold that behaviourism exerted for so long on psychology and opened the way for the greater, albeit baffling, complexities of non-linear systems. The Nobel Prize winner Roger Sperry, originally a dedicated reductionist, now argues:

> According to traditional atomistic or microdeterministic science, everything is determined from below upwards follow-ing the course of evolution. Brain states determine mental states, but not vice versa. In the new view, however, things are doubly determined, not only from the lower levels upward, but also from above downward.
>
> (Sperry, quoted in Tresan 1996)

Francis Crick, another Nobel laureate formerly committed to reductionism, now accepts that subjective experience cannot be totally explained in terms of neurological events, and concedes that 'much of the behaviour of the brain is emergent'.

'The doctrine of emergence', explains philosopher Donald Davidson, 'is the claim that when basic physicochemical processes achieve a certain level of complexity of an appropriate kind, genuinely novel characteristics such as mentality, appear as "emergent" qualities' (quoted in Tresan 1996).

Complementary with emergentism is the current idea of 'supervenience', which suggests that phenomena are influenced from above by mental forces (such as values) as much as from below by material forces. In brief, mental forces supervene while material ones subvene.

The theories of emergentism and supervenience endeavour to explain the anomalies of evolution up to high levels of consciousness without recourse to the concept of a superordinate being. From time immemorial people have subscribed to the notion of a pre-existing power that originally generated the world and still sustains it. It was clearly articulated, for example, by the philosopher Socrates, who claimed that Absolute Truth along with Absolute Beauty, Absolute Goodness and the like exist from the beginning and are themselves the foundation of all that has come into being. Socrates' 'absolutes' are ideas that enjoy an existence independent of anyone who might think them. 'The truth, or true thought', says Bion, 'does not require a thinker – he is not logically necessary' (Bion 1970: 102).

This is contrary to the common-sense assumptions of classical science which says: 'Here is the material world we live in; we can see it and touch it; it is the basis of our existence; from simple material ingredients all life has evolved, climbing up the evolutionary ladder to man, who has a brain at the top of his body which produces thoughts.' This is the position which Freud assumed in his understanding of the development of consciousness: from the body came the primary instincts which manifested as a power he called the id, from the id came the ego, and with the ego the capacity for thought.

Now the idealist view turns this picture upside down. It claims that before all else there is consciousness; originally whole, pure, perfect, totally self-contained in the eternal present; otherwise called Mind, the Godhead, the Absolute, the 'Ein Sof'. Consciousness is not waiting for the development of the physical brain but is prior to it; the brain is itself an expression of it. Consciousness exists from the beginning. It exists, but in order to become *manifest* it must divide into a knower and that which is known. This is the primary split into self and other, the first Fall, the Original Sin; a notion that readily lends itself to biblical terminology, because it is simply a restatement of God dividing light from darkness. From this first split further splits follow: between life and death, past and future, mind and body, conscious and unconscious. From the non-materialist perspective this originally non-dual conscious-ness now exists in a whole spectrum of

> mutually penetrating forms of energy, from the finest 'all radiating', all pervading luminous consciousness down to the densest form of 'materialised' consciousness which appears before us as our physical body.
>
> (Govinda 1973: 148)

Mind is not refined matter: matter is dense consciousness – or more likely some unknown reality that transcends both. The movement is not from below upwards but from above down-wards, or possibly up and down at the same time, a view similar to that of supervenience. Mind was there in the beginning and is here now; our task is to break through the delusions of everyday consciousness to reach it. Since this non-material, non-dual reality is, by definition, without attributes, common sense tends all too readily to equate it with nothingness. But those, like the Buddha, who have gained direct access to it assure us that pure conscious-ness is a realm of infinite and indescribable richness.

> Verily there is a realm where there is neither the solid nor the fluid, neither heat nor motion, neither this world nor the other world, neither sun nor moon. . . . There is, O monks, an Unborn, Unoriginated, Uncreated, Unformed. If there were not this Unborn, Unoriginated, Uncreated, Unformed, escape from the world of the born, the originated, the created, the formed would not be possible.
>
> (quoted in Conze 1938)

Compared to the reality of non-dual consciousness the three-dimensional version of reality offered by normal waking con-sciousness is an inferior derivative, and can perhaps be likened to a dream. This implies that we are all, for the greater part of our lives, asleep. There is an obvious difficulty in accepting such a viewpoint, since the dreamer only knows he is dreaming when he actually wakes up; while he is dreaming he does not know he is in a dream. The implications of what contemporary science has discovered are that until we each wake up, even for a moment, we will persist in the delusion of believing in the exclusive and objective reality of the common-sense world we perceive around us.

Chapter 6

New science and psychotherapy

If the twentieth-century scientific viewpoint reinstates conscious-ness as an essential ingredient in existence, if it allows subjectivity some degree of objectivity, this has profound implications for the future of psychotherapy. It is an irony that the validation psycho-analysis was denied by classical science, because of its subjective bias and its failure to make accurate predictions, can now be conferred by the new science of the twentieth century. Subjectivity has ceased to be a pejorative term but has become admissible evidence, part of a more complex definition of truth that involves neither the scientific dogma of objectivity nor the distorting bias of subjectivity. If the effect of the human observer has been detected even in the remote zones of nuclear physics, how much more must its relevance apply to human concerns?

My own limited observations that the interactions taking place in psychotherapy cannot be satisfactorily described in linear terms have been noted by a number of psychotherapy practitioners, among whom one of the earliest was Jung:

> The way is not straight but appears to go round in circles. More accurate knowledge proved it to go round in spirals . . . we can hardly help feeling that the unconscious process moves spiral wise round a centre, gradually getting closer, while the characteristics of the centre grow more and more distinct.
>
> (Jung 1944: para. 35)

More recently Zinkin published an innovative paper applying holography to analytic psychology:

> My own belief is that the hologram provides a new way of clarifying the most confusing and contradictory concepts in

Jung's thought, the nature of psyche, the collective unconscious, the archetypes and individuation.

(Zinkin 1987)

The goal of individuation is to become whole. In Jung's view this
goal is unattainable, which means that everyone is incomplete; not
the incompleteness of 'not being all there', but the existential
incompleteness of always moving towards completeness. The
essence of individuation is movement. In Bohm's view, movement
is primary, while the discrete entities of the phenomenal world as
they emerge from the holomovement are secondary. Zinkin notes:

> Bohm often gives the example of the vortex, or the ripple in
> water, as an analogy for this kind of relatively stable entity
> which is indivisible. The water is in the vortex and the vortex is
> in the water. Perhaps, like the vortex, the self unfolds and is then
> folded back. . . .

(Zinkin 1987)

An earlier paper by Edgar Levenson also found profound
analogies between holography and the analytic process: psychoanalysis, as currently practised, correctly assumes that every
aspect of the patient's life, the material he presents, his relationship with the analyst are all of a piece: in a word, the analytic
relationship is essentially holographic.

> any small piece of the clinical material contains the total
> configuration. Both past and future. Thus the patient's opening
> comment in the waiting room or coming in the door or as he sits
> in the chair, will establish the leitmotif that runs through the
> entire session, that picks up the last session, and will very likely
> continue on into the next session. Any ten minutes of a taped
> session can be explicated to an entire analysis. Any dream of the
> patient contains implicit in it – literally, enfolded in it – the
> entire story of the patient's neurotic difficulties.

(Levenson 1976: 2–3)

Levenson comments on the disparity between the apparent clarity
of analytic theory and the confusion of the analyst's actual
experience:

> Although we all get clinical results with our patients we would
> be hard put often to say exactly what it is we do that makes the
> difference. . . . Sudden or insidious, dramatic or by default,

change does not come at the behest of any technique or procedure. If his life depended on it, no therapist could produce a therapeutic result on command. In fact the more his life depended on it, the less likely he would be to produce a therapeutic result. . . . In this, psychoanalysis fails to meet the expectations of scientific enquiry.

(Levenson 1976: 2–3)

Levenson is only one of a number of psychoanalysts who have questioned the adequacy of linear causation. Although other psychotherapeutic approaches, such as *Gestalt*, psychosynthesis, transpersonal and existentialist psychology have long subscribed to a holistic model, classical psychoanalysis has been inclined to view these 'alternative' approaches as lacking in both clinical rigour and scientific credibility. More recently the psychoanalyst Margaret Arden has written on David Bohm's ideas and their implications for a religious view of life, compared with Freud's rationalistic position which treated religion as a collective obsessional neurosis. She notes that Bohm's juxtaposition of the implicate and explicate orders echoes Freud's primary and secondary processes, but whereas Freud emphasised secondary process Bohm treats primary process as fundamental. In discussing the psychoanalyst Matte Blanco she notes that his concept of multi-dimensional space 'is virtually the same as Bohm's concept of the infinite dimensionality of the holomovement' (Arden 1993: 151). She summarises her position by saying:

I have become increasingly convinced that the so-called scientific attitude in psychoanalysis is a serious limitation. . . . I want to suggest that the transference relationship with the analyst as good parent engenders a healing process which exists in its own right. If we think about mental processes as analogous to physical processes, we can suppose there is a natural healing tendency in the mind which corresponds to the healing of physical wounds. The separation of mind and body is no longer tenable.

(Arden 1993)

With each advance in neuroscience the brain emerges as an ever more extraordinary organ:

There are probably fifty to five hundred kinds of neurons in the cortex alone and in the entire brain the number of neurons is in the order of ten to one hundred billion. Moreover, each neuron has an axon which may have up to ten thousand synaptic connections, and each synapse, in turn, has untold numbers (probably millions) of physical, molecular, and chemical events that occur at all levels ... the permutations in just one human brain exceed 10 to the 100 trillion, a number which if written out with all its zeros would fill all imaginable space ... the encounter of one brain with another, as in analysis, squares the number of possible variables.

(Tresan 1996)

Since the brain is of such a complex and fluid nature the evidence indicates that any significant experience redistributes synapses and reinforces neural pathways; even just talking actually changes its anatomy; it follows that after therapeutic treatment the very brain of a patient is different.

But it would seem that the experience needs to reach a certain level of intensity and to have meaning for the subject to produce measurable changes in the cortex. But once this occurs 'the cortical mapping of all similar past experiences is reconfigured in that portion of the brain. In other words, all learning is interrelated, and one learned fact alters all knowledge' (Tresan 1996).

The factors of *meaning* and *intensity* have profound implications for therapeutic technique. Unless patient and therapist are emotionally engaged change cannot happen; hence the emphasis on the power of transference, trust and spontaneity. Merely studied, cerebral interpretations, however correct, have no effect. But interventions must also address the patient's area of concern, hence the necessity for empathic listening. Moreover change does not occur in isolation but changes the anatomy over a broad area. Mathematically based research into non-linear systems was initiated by the 'catastrophe theories' of Thom. He demonstrated how relatively minute causes in the natural world can escalate to produce massive outcomes in distant places. In the now familiar metaphor: a butterfly opens its wings in, say, Tokyo and produces a storm in Los Angeles. This is one of the defining characteristics of chaotic dynamics, known as SDIC – sensitive dependence on initial conditions. Chaotic dynamics never retrace the same path twice (unlike a pendulum), even though they follow recognisable patterns. These patterns are called strange attractors. They constitute: 'the epitome of contradiction, never repeating, yet always resembling itself; infinitely recognisable, never predictable' (Van Eenwyck 1991: 7).

Precisely the same description can be applied to our notion of self. Thom's ideas were picked up by the psychoanalyst Galatzer-Levy who applied catastrophe theory to plot hitherto unpredictable shifts both in psychological breakdown and recovery. But it has also been of interest to Jungian analysts:

> when the tension between consciousness and the unconscious reaches a certain critical value . . . chaos enters the psychic realm (bifurcations and period doubling). This leads to a psychic situation that consciousness finds it virtually impossible to differentiate. Yet, if the chaos is allowed to continue (the tension of opposites maintained), recognisable patterns (symbols/ fractal attractors) eventually appear. These patterns represent the emergence of order from chaos.
>
> (Van Eenwyck 1991: 9)

One of the most recent and ambitious projects to apply mathematical models to psychological processes is being attempted by Robert Langs.

> Psychotherapy and psychoanalysis appear to be far closer to forms of intermittent turbulence and uncertainty than to ordered systems . . . one of the goals of mathematical modelling is to discover the underlying order beneath the surface chaos of the psychotherapeutic interaction.
>
> (Langs 1988: 206)

Langs differentiates between chaotic systems and those which are cyclic or oscillating. Whereas the latter would apply to fluctuations in the wellbeing of basically healthy individuals, the unexpected creation of order out of chaos would better apply to the breakdown–breakthrough pattern described in this book. Langs is attempting to plot the course of communicative exchanges between analyst and patient according to non-linear models. Although theoretically possible, given the SDIC factor, it seems doubtful if such an intellectually heroic endeavour could be usefully employed in clinical work.

All the analysts referred to above (plus many authors quoted by them but not reproduced here) broadly subscribe to what Levenson calls 'a radically new paradigm' (1976: 19). And yet it is not wholly new. If we study the ferment of creative ideas engendered between Freud, Jung and Ferenczi in the early years of this century – involving mutual analysis, unconscious and psychic influence, the mysterious interaction of psyche and soma – we see that they speculate on many of the themes explored in this chapter. The difference lies in the fact that advances in knowledge since that time – for example that each new *thought* physically changes the structure of the brain – give greater substance to what were no more than exciting speculations.

As we approach the twenty-first century acceptance of this new paradigm may be a little nearer, but is by no means imminent. It probably took the whole of the seventeenth century and well beyond to convince the general public that the world was round and not flat. It may take even longer for the radical implications of modern science to modify the common-sense assumptions by which we currently live.

Chapter 7

The spectrum of consciousness

If the sun happens to shine through a storm cloud we might be lucky enough to see a rainbow. The different colours of the rainbow, each vibrating at a different wave length, comprise the spectrum which makes up white light. Consciousness likewise comprises a spectrum of different levels ranging from the simple to the complex. In fact whatever exists, whether mind or matter, is hierarchically ordered: a living body is a set of interdependent subsystems of limbs and organs. The same applies to any form of social organisation, whether it is the civil service or a colony or ants. Any solid substance can be reduced to molecules, molecules to atoms, atoms to particles, and down through the sub-atomic spectrum to the non-material energy network that underpins all existence. How is this energy to be conceived?

In the system propounded by Plotinus, the neo-Platonic philosopher who wrote and taught around the beginning of the Christian era, the cosmos originates from the 'One' in a series of descending emanations. The first he calls Intelligence (not just human intelligence but the mind of God), from which in turn issues the Soul, and from Soul is born the lowest manifestation which is Matter. Like the rays of the sun, these emanations grow dimmer with distance from the 'One', culminating in total darkness, or non-being (Inge 1929). The twentieth-century Hindu philosopher Sri Aurobindo likewise envisaged a descending four-step hierarchy, beginning with 'the inactive Brahman, the transcendent Silence' down through Mind, Life, and finally Matter (Stace 1960). Ken Wilber, a contemporary Western philosopher, speaks of an 'all-inclusive yet dimensionless reality of which each level represents an illusory deviation'. The evolution of what he calls the spectrum of consciousness is described thus:

In reality, there is Mind-only, the 'all-inclusive', non-dual, the timeless ground of all temporal phenomena, 'fusion without confusion', a Reality 'without duality but not without relations'. . . . But through the process of *maya*, of dualistic thought, we introduce illusory dualities or divisions, 'creating two worlds from one'. These divisions are not real, but only seeming, yet man behaves in every way *as if* they were real; and being thus duped, man clings to his first and primordial dualism, that of subject vs. object, self vs. not-self, or simply organism vs. environment. At this point, man shifts from a cosmic identity with the All to a personal identity with his organism, and we thus generate a second major level of consciousness, the Existential Level: man identified with his organism.

Like an ascending spiral, man's fragmentation through duality continues, so that most individuals don't even feel identified with all of their organism – we say not 'I am a body' but rather 'I *have* a body', and this 'I' that '*has*' a body we call our self, our *ego*. At this point, man's identity shifts from his organism as a whole to his ego, and we have generated a third major level of consciousness, the Ego Level. Continuing this dualistic spiral, man can even attempt to disown facets of his ego that he finds undesirable, refusing to admit into his consciousness the unwanted aspects of himself.

(Wilber 1977: 4–6; emphasis in original)

Jung likewise posits four realms that supervene one on another: the mineral world, the plant world, the animal world, and ultimately the spiritual world. In the hierarchy of the ancient Greek religion Zeus was the supreme deity; immediately below him were the lesser gods, Titans, centaurs, and a vast panoply of spirits all subject to his rule; below these came the human species, and below that the animal, vegetable and mineral kingdoms. In the Judaeo-Christian tradition heaven is located above with all its angels, hell below with all its demons, with earth sandwiched in between.

The hierarchical image of the cosmos reflects the nature and structure of man himself: the upper half of the body has always denoted the higher centres of head and heart while the lower half takes care of the sexual and excretory functions. Jewish mysticism of the Kabalah depicts man in terms of the Tree of Life, with its roots reaching into the soil and its branches rooted in heaven. The chakra system of the East identifies various levels of consciousness, each with its specific psychological characteristics. These begin from the lowest centre below the genitals, rising up the spine to the sexual centre, then to the spleen, navel, heart, throat, culminating in the head. The chakra system locates these 'haras' or zones in the *subtle* body, which are not to be concretely identified with physical organs. The theosophical system, closely corresponding to the chakras, envisages successive 'subtle bodies' which ascend from the physical up through the astral, mental, etheric and finally spiritual modes of apprehension. The psychoanalytic concept of *internal objects*, as well as the ego, the id and the superego, could all be said to have, like the chakras, a 'subtle' status; that is, they cannot be identified physically but act as centres of energy.

Contemporary versions of hierarchical levels of consciousness were proposed by Freud and his followers in delineating the oral, anal, phallic and genital stages in human development. Like the chakras, these stages are correlated with body zones, but given a different order of priority. Freud emphasised the sexual drive, identified with the genital area. Melanie Klein focused on the breast, which probably corresponds to the heart centre. Meltzer has shown a special interest in the bowel area; more precisely in the hypothetical bowel of the 'internalised mother', which he connects with seriously pathological states. Something of the same body–mind correspondence can be found in demonology, since the demons too were thought to take up residence in different zones of the body.

The differentiation of levels of consciousness has been noted by most contemporary psychologists. Freud, as we have seen, distinguished primary from secondary process (Freud 1916–17); Melanie Klein focused on the difference between the 'paranoid-schizoid' and the 'depressive' positions (Klein 1957); Jung differentiates the archetypal unconscious, the personal unconscious, the ego (which he regards as a 'complex'), the symbolic, all leading to the spiritual or transpersonal levels of experience.

Daniel Stern plots four successive stages in the development of the normal infant's sense of self: these he terms the emergent self, the core self, the subjective self and the verbal self. Lacan differentiates three levels of development which he terms the Real, corresponding to primary experience, the Imaginary, with an emphasis on false-self experience, and the Symbolic, which equates with Freud's secondary process and puts great store on language. Maslow differentiates D-Motivation, dominated by deficiency; B-Motivation, characterised by the urge for self-realisation; leading to the Transpersonal, which may include peak experiences. Wilber differentiates the 'eye of flesh' from the 'eye of reason' and culminating in the 'eye of contemplation' (Wilber 1990: 4–6).

In accord with the foregoing, I have chosen to differentiate a four-step hierarchy. The first three will be readily recognisable, the fourth rather more problematic. Whether the four-dimensional state leads to still higher developmental levels is hypothetically feasible but purely speculative. These higher levels may be compared to a small blur of light barely discernible on the outer edge of the cosmos; with more powerful telescopes it may turn out to be an entirely new universe immeasurably greater than our own, but as yet it remains beyond our vision.

ONE DIMENSIONALITY

The way that very young children experience their existence is profoundly different from that of adults, and any attempt to delineate a one-dimensional world must involve a measure of speculative reconstruction. But since it was a world that each of us once inhabited, perhaps some vestiges of it can still be glimpsed in memory. The opening words of James Joyce's autobiographical novel *Portrait of the Artist as a Young Man* convey something of the primitive immediacy of infant experience: 'First it was warm, then it was cold.' This is presumably how it feels to soil a nappy. Joyce especially catches the stunning simplicity of infant emotion where warm is good, cold is bad; where full is good, empty is bad; where pleasure is good, pain is bad. The focus of infant awareness is located in certain physical areas: the skin, the mouth, and the inside of the body which may be comfortably full, painfully distended or agonisingly empty.

In his description of autistic children Donald Meltzer refers to 'a one-dimensional world, which we have characterised as substantially mindless, consisting of a series of events not available for memory or thought.... Gratification and fusion with the object would be undifferentiated' (Meltzer 1975: 69ff.). This original state of non-differentiation Freud called primary narcissism, Mahler calls it autism, Kohut hypothesises an initial state he calls 'self-object', which is intended to convey that subject and object are merged in a single experience. More recently Thomas Ogden has described a state prior to Melanie Klein's 'schizoid-paranoid position' which he calls 'autistic-contiguous'.

It is likely that infant awareness is confined to physical sensations; thus emotions such as frustration or fear would be experienced as bodily pain. By definition there can be no conflict, only an alternation between satiation and deficit. Matte Blanco regards primary process as dominated by 'symmetrical thinking', a non-logical type of thought where the part is equal to the whole. Thus if there is pain, the world is composed only of pain. Even when some degree of differentiation has taken place and the infant's mother is recognised as something other than itself, if she is absent for too long, or a feed is too slow in coming, it is as if she is gone for ever, and life stops. This type of thinking is readily revived in adults in times of strong emotion.

Another source of speculation about primitive experience comes from physiological research. This indicates that:

> the neuronal connections of an infant's cerebral cortex are lacking in the level of myelination and are immature in a variety of other respects – observations which have led to the conclusion that infants are essentially precorticate. On the psychological level, depth psychologists and developmental theorists alike suggest that the perceptions and cognitions of human infants only gradually, and in tandem with their physiological growth, demonstrate differentiation and categorisation of experience, and that neonates are characterised initially by a lack of ego boundaries. At a very early stage in the infant's life (and before it, in the life of the fetus) a fused, synesthetic mode may be naturally present and expressed in kinesthetic activity as the infant (or fetus) relates to an as yet undifferentiated universe.
>
> (Mavromatis 1987: 267)

If it takes a certain length of time after birth before the cortex of the brain becomes fully operative – it has been suggested that full myelination does not occur until a child is into the Oedipal phase – the main mental activity of infants may be presumed to derive from the old and mid-brain centres. The one-dimensional level of mental functioning corresponds to Freud's 'primary process'. This he saw as the expression of an impersonal life force he called the id whose single aim was the pursuit of pleasure by means of the release of psychic tension. Although Freud's id is essentially a functional construct and not a material entity, it could well correspond anatomically with the sub-cortical areas of the brain. Animals are conscious, but not conscious of themselves in the way that humans are, and presumably very early infant experience functions on the same level. But animals, unlike newly born human infants, do show a capacity for thinking and memory in hunting prey or evading predators.

Some adult approximation to primary experience may be found in dreams, which Freud saw 'as remnants of the supremacy of [the pleasure] principle and proofs of its power' (Freud 1925: 14). Dreams also provide the experience where the different senses themselves may be undifferentiated, so that sounds might have a taste or a colour, sight will include the quality of touch, and so on. Mavromatis reports that similar synaesthetic experience commonly occurs in hypnagogia, as well as in psychotic, hypnotic, meditative, creative and mystical states where the different senses may be conflated and virtually impossible to translate into words. This leads to the intriguing speculation that before the differentiating cortex came into operation, we originally had a single undifferentiated sense; so that taste, sight, touch, smell and sound constituted one unified experience. Some derivative of the conflation of the senses is retained in a vast variety of metaphorical expressions such as a 'silky sound' or a 'delectable sight'. There is no reason to assume that these primitive types of apprehension ever atrophy but are simply repressed. Composers such as Olivier Messaien and Scriabin were among many who had the clearest sense that every sound has its specific colour.

In a dimension where there is no ego there can be no ego boundaries, and communication is direct and unmediated. Amongst living creatures this can be seen, for example, in flocks of birds which wheel and turn as if they were constituent parts of a single organism. The same applies to the nest-building activities of ants, each of whom acts as if directed by a higher consciousness. In so far as 'neonates are characterised initially by a lack of ego boundaries' (Mavromatis 1987: 242–3) and normal mothers are abnormally sensitised towards their newborn infants, this may account for the direct, seemingly unmediated communication that can occur between them. I suspect that in my sessions with

Yvonne, where her primitive erotic feelings infiltrated my ego boundaries, much of our interaction took place at this one-dimensional level.

A somewhat different picture of the mind of a newborn infant is presented by Daniel Stern. He adopts an interpersonal standpoint and measures development not in Freud's terms of ego and id but of that equally hypothetical entity he calls the self. He insists that experimental and observational studies indicate that infants 'never experience a period of total self/other undifferentiation. There is no confusion between self and other in the beginning or at any point during infancy' (Stern 1985: 43–4). Support for his view comes from the newest techniques in observing the active life of the foetus while still in the womb, where indications of a specific innate personality are readily identifiable. In tracing the evolution of the sense of self through its four stages, Stern makes the important point that they do not simply follow one another or become permanently resolved. Although each stage is the foundation for its successor, it is not swallowed up by it, and remains active throughout adult life.

Between Freud's hypothesis of primary narcissism, which envisages a state where everything is in the self, and the object relations theory which regards the notion of a self without an object as unthinkable, there exists a serious epistemological gulf. Of course, it does not follow that, because a state is *unthinkable*, it cannot exist. The object relations theorist would argue that if there exists no 'other' that the self knows, it would follow that there is no sense *either* of self *or* other – that knowledge and non-differentiation cannot coexist. It is necessary that this divergence should be acknowledged, although I can offer no logical solution to it.

TWO DIMENSIONALITY

The one-dimensional level is popularly conveyed by the term 'one-track mind'. It evokes the image of a train that can only move back and forth in a straight line – whereas a ship can take any course across the surface of the sea and therefore moves in two dimensions. The ship, in turn, differs from a submarine which can also explore the depths: namely, it can move in three dimensions. Three dimensionality in psychological terms is the equivalent of Freud's 'secondary' process. What I call two-dimensional consciousness lies somewhere between the first and the third and overlaps both. Balint gives an engaging clinical picture of the two-dimensional level of functioning; although he terms it the 'area of basic fault' he is also precisely describing Melanie Klein's paranoid-schizoid position:

> interpretations given by the analyst are not experienced any longer by the patient as interpretations. Instead he may feel them as an attack, a demand, a base insinuation, an uncalled-for rudeness or insult, unfair treatment, or at least a complete lack of consideration, and so on. . . . If now the analyst fails to 'click in' , that is to respond as the patient expects him to, no reaction of anger, rage, contempt, or criticism will appear in the transference as one would expect it at the Oedipal level. The only thing that can be observed is a feeling of emptiness, being lost, deadness, futility, and so on.
>
> (Balint 1968: 19)

Balint's basic fault also includes one-dimensional phenomena:

> Moreover – and this is not so easy to admit – the patient somehow seems able to get under the analyst's skin. He begins to know too much about his analyst. This increase in knowledge does not originate in any outside source of information but apparently from an uncanny talent that enables the patient to 'understand' the analyst's motives and to 'interpret' his behaviour. This uncanny talent may occasionally give the impression of, or perhaps even amount to, telepathy or clairvoyance.
>
> (Balint 1968: 20)

Meltzer suggests that where the significance of objects is inseparable from their sensual qualities, the sense of self is possibly experienced very much as a sensitive surface. This links with Esther Bick's idea that the infantile ego can be compared to the skin, the main function of which is to control what gets in and what gets out. Thus in schizoid personalities emotions appear to be no more than 'skin deep'. There may be a great deal of surface drama, passionate declarations, threats, violent or hysterical gestures but the observer remains strangely untouched, even alienated. In the realm of the two dimensional there seems to be no inner space. As we encounter it in the analytic situation we find that helpful interpretations can find nowhere in which to sink; they just drain away, like rain off plate glass. Thinking at this level is predominantly concrete, with little sense of 'as if'. A common exchange might go as follows:

Therapist: Say you did win the lottery (pass the exam, find a partner, etc.), what would you...?
Patient: Well, I *haven't*, have I?

Two-dimensional consciousness could be thought of as equivalent to a flat earth mentality. The two-dimensional personality lives only at the fixed centre of a psychologically flat, private world and suffers an underlying fear of 'going over the edge'. And just as the spherical shape of the earth's surface becomes distorted when reduced to a map, at the two-dimensional paranoid level there occurs an equivalent emotional distortion of the world and the people in it.

A two-dimensional surface not only extends across an area, but like a coin, can also be imagined as having a top and a bottom. This reintroduces the notion of opposites, the most fundamental of which is the discrimination between self and other. The shift from the first to the second dimension involves the crucial move into discrimination and thence to language. But at this stage two-dimensional thoughts and feelings, like Jung's archetypes, can only be of a polarised kind, with clear-cut distinctions between good and bad, right and wrong. Thus it is the realm of passionate convictions, albeit short-lived: 'the worst', as Yeats said, 'are full of a passionate intensity' (1933).

Since heads and tails are simply two sides of the same coin, they are also uncomfortably close. Love can readily turn to hatred, bliss to boredom, desire to revulsion. The two-dimensional character is either omnipotent or impotent, bully or victim, manic or depressed, gullible or paranoid. Each state, while it has possession of consciousness, imposes its own reality and totally excludes its opposite. Depressed, I can hardly remember even a moment of happiness. If I am in love, I love with the whole of my being and in my beloved there can be no blemish. Curiously enough, this kind of idealisation all too often passes for true love. But if a single defect is discovered then that love is utterly nullified. It needs just one failing and a hundred kindnesses are instantly wiped out.

In the two-dimensional state we cannot be self-possessed because our moods possess us. Even if we are possessed by elation, the sense of not being in control gives it a horrible flavour, like a mouthful of saccharine. This may underlie the fear many people have of allowing themselves to be truly happy: they all too readily become manic, which may be the nearest state to happiness they have experienced. To avoid mania they avoid situations which might prove truly joyful, or they spoil it for themselves immediately afterwards by persecutory ruminations. They find it difficult to enjoy what they have while they have it but grieve intensely if they should lose it. In the two-dimensional state our hurts hurt more than our pleasures please.

The rapid alternation of contrasting states of mind evokes, at its worst, a sickening sense of instability, as if there is no centre, no one at home, the feeling one could 'crack up' at any moment and bits of oneself could fly off in any direction. But one and two dimensionality also constitute the main source of energy and passion, and without it life becomes merely cerebral and sterile. Plato likened the human condition to a horse and rider: without the horse the rider goes nowhere. Two-dimensional characters are often exciting to have around. Since their reactions are never predictable, there is always something going on with them; and this is how they try to keep meaninglessness at bay. They may shout, shriek, weep; none of it carries much conviction, yet their pain is real. Although they do a great deal of acting, they act the truth.

Politics, news and entertainment are all deeply contaminated by two dimensionality: shock headlines, whether true or false, sell newspapers. The heroes of the entertainment world embody the general desire for ever more excitement; their fate is to be adored one day and vilified the next. In the political arena, reasoned opinions readily degenerate into convictions; doubt and complexity are difficult to sustain and rapidly harden into dead certainties. Hence the millions passionately devoted to fundamentalist religious and political beliefs which relieve them from the torments of ambivalence and indecision. A nation at war, especially civil war, is one sunk in two dimensionality. The enemy – who only yesterday may have been a neighbour – is now, by definition, the embodiment of unredeemed evil. To defeat the enemy, every lie, every atrocity, is justified, which, in turn, perpetuates a virtually unbreakable cycle of hatred and revenge. The hatred extends not only towards the perpetrator of a specific misdeed, but to everyone connected with them: their family and entire community. Here the one dimensional prevails over the two dimensional; the reptilian brain is in control and uses the higher functions for its own purposes. Hence it is a form of behaviour peculiar to humans and unthinkable in animals. Under the dominance of symmetrical thinking there is no distinction drawn between the part and the whole, thereby providing the justification for the wholesale murder and violation of innocent people, simply because they belong to the same religion, tribe or family of the current enemy. Diplomacy and negotiation are attempts to lift human interaction to the three-dimensional level; but all too often these are disguised one-dimensional manoeuvres.

Most personal behaviour is conducted in terms of conformity to the norm, where things are either permitted or forbidden. Individuals, and especially groups, view life more or less in terms of black or white, friend or enemy, truth and falsehood. The great two-dimensional virtues are unwavering loyalty, uncompromising rectitude, unquestioning obedience. It is the basis on which most societies rest. Family bonding rarely goes beyond the two-dimensional level and what passes for love is more usually symbiotic attachment between couples, or the narcissistic identification of parents with their children. These ties preclude all questioning, and therefore possess immense strength.

The same strength is manifest in two-dimensional characters: they will readily die for an ideology, territory, nation or family; some have even killed for their local football team. They often gain positions of power since their certainty carries great conviction; society turns to them in times of crisis and makes them into leaders. It is a cruel irony that those who are most deeply split all too often achieve positions of the greatest political power. Whether we like it or not, the 'real world' of jobs, money, sexuality, status, family, dynasty and state is dominated and permeated by two dimensionality.

THREE DIMENSIONALITY

Here we enter the familiar territory of so-called normal experience, which Freud called secondary process. 'A new principle of mental functioning was introduced: what was conceived of was no longer that which was pleasant, but that which was real, even if it should be unpleasant' (Freud 1925: 14). This involved the development of certain faculties such as attention, notation, memory, judgement and, ultimately, thought. The combination of all these functions constitutes the ego.

Elaborating on Freud's view that the ego is fundamentally a 'body ego', Meltzer connects this process with the development in the infant of the conception of 'orifices in the object or self ... which can only be realised once a sphincter function had become effective' (Meltzer 1975: 224–6). He regards the capacity of the infant to control and protect its own orifices as a precondition for the self to conceive of an inner or 'potential' space. With the notion of inner space, or the differentiation of inside from outside, we have left the 'flatland' of two dimensionality and entered the third dimension. Through the combination of the first and second dimensions a new dimension has emerged; the opposites have combined into something more than the sum of the constituent parts, rather as hydrogen and oxygen, in themselves insubstantial gases, combine to form water.

The three dimensional represents all that civilised society holds dear: rationality, balance, adulthood, fairness, flexibility, restraint, the ability to listen and to respect the integrity of another. The intellectual faculty combines with our primary instincts to produce the capacity for imagination, metaphor and symbolisation, which are the basic requirements of all creative endeavour. Freud felt that in science, characterised by objectivity and a love of truth, could be found the highest expression of secondary process. Whereas two dimensionality is marked by polarity and conviction, the three dimensional is searching, reflective, ambivalent. Mindful of the loss of infantile omnipotence, Melanie Klein termed it the 'depressive position'.

In the clinical situation, when a patient makes a shift from two to three dimensionality it is not always easy to define what is happening. Their external circumstances may remain much the same; they may stay with the same partner, and carry on doing much the same things as before, except that there is an altogether different feel about them. They have become more 'rounded personalities'; they feel easier and safer to handle; it is possible to be involved with them but not so entangled. They have a resilience that can take everyday knocks without cracking up. There is now a space inside where thought can take place, where insights can be held. Their capacity for reflection inhibits impulsive action and obsessive thinking; there is a new-found freedom from chronic inner persecution, experienced as an obscure but deep sense of wrongness and badness. Above all, they have a different feeling about *themselves*; they find that life goes more slowly, is somewhat less exciting but far more rewarding.

This holds good even when life goes badly. I recall one patient who came to therapy to cope with the death of a child. What tormented her most was not only the suffering her loss entailed but an indescribable sense of numbness, as if she had lost her feeling self. If her grief could actually be reached in the session she welcomed it, since with her tears came both the renewed presence of her lost child and of *herself*, however deeply sorrowful. The same could be said of my patient Elaine who felt she could cope with a life full of disappointment and frustration because now she was a 'person'. The shift from two to three dimensionality is one whose significance cannot be overestimated. Freud understood this in his wry comment that the best psychoanalysis can do is to convert neurotic misery into common human unhappiness (1925: 305). This was the limit his scepticism allowed him to go. Dare we envisage that depth psychology might possibly do more?

Chapter 8

The fourth dimension

Is it possible to imagine a four-dimensional geometrical structure?

> It is very hard to visualise such a dimension directly. Off and on for some fifteen years, I have tried to do so. In all this time I've managed a grand total of some fifteen minutes' worth of direct vision into four-dimensional space. Nevertheless I feel I understand the fourth dimension very well. How can this be? How can we talk productively about something that is almost impossible to visualise? The key idea is by analogy. The fourth dimension is to three-dimensional space as the third dimension is to two-dimensional space.
>
> (Rucker 1994: 7–8)

If we apply the notion of dimensionality to levels of personal development we can say that each dimension encompasses its predecessor. In this sense the child is father to the man, and the infant father to the child. In order to envisage psychological four dimensionality we must resort to Rucker's expedient of analogy. In his allegory of the cave Plato imagined a race of men chained together underground where they could see only their own shadows on the wall facing them. Knowing no other reality, they failed to realise that these shadows were mere outlines of their own three-dimensional bodies of which they were hardly aware. Plato's story tries to tell us that we think we live in daylight when actually we live in darkness, and that we are all prisoners of our own enchained perception which presents us to ourselves as mere shadows of what we really are.

It may be objected that to apply to psychology the geometrical notion of dimensionality is to conflate different categories of knowledge. Yet Einstein himself audaciously broke open the categories of space and time when he joined them into a four-dimensional concept of 'space–time'. The psychological equivalent would be states of 'self–other'. This is by no means so rare as may be supposed. A direct sense of what the other is thinking or feeling is not unusual between a mother and her baby, between twins, members of the same family, partners, lovers, friends and, not least, enemies. Some types of people are unusually open to self–other awareness: this includes not only clairvoyants and psychics but also those who suffer mental disturbance. Balint noted that patients functioning at the 'basic fault' level have the capacity to get under the therapist's skin. In my experience a paranoid member of a therapy group will prove acutely sensitive to the minutest sniff of repressed hostility coming from any quarter of the room. In the individual therapy situation a patient may challenge me: 'Why are you so angry?' My first reaction is surprise because I don't feel in the least bit angry, but a bit more reflection and I glimpse they may just be right, as if they can smell it. But this kind of direct knowing, which we share with many simpler life forms, does not qualify as four-dimensional since it constitutes a primary fusion in which the sense of both self and other is diminished or lost.

One of the ways in which the four-dimensional state can be experienced is the *simultaneous union and separation of self and other*. I have in mind those moments where two people feel profoundly united with one another yet each retains a singularly enriched sense of themselves. We are not lost in the other, as in fusion, but found. John Haule says that there 'seems to be a transpersonal, autonomous, directing intelligence, mutual to the two partners, somehow constituted by their union, and yet not reducible to either nor directly manipulable' (Haule 1990: 210–11).

Whether shared, or experienced in solitude, the four-dimensional state is one that many people have known and tried to convey in art, music, poetry, and, most especially, in the paradoxical utterances of mystical literature. Maslow calls it 'peak experience' and Bollas 'aesthetic experience', both of which are highly positive manifestations. But under the broad heading of altered states of consciousness we need to recognise the therapeutic potential of both negative and positive states: hence my emphasis on breakdown.

The hypothesis that a profound and intense psychedelic experience, regardless of its emotional valence, can serve as a catalyst for rapid personal growth is consistent with current interpretations of both nadir and peak experiences. Concerning nadir experiences, Erikson's brilliant analysis of the post-adolescent identity crisis has recently been extended to include periodic 'crises of maturation' (Erikson), naturally occurring 'desolation experiences' (Laski) and the therapeutic value of 'existential crises' (Bugental).

(Mogar 1965: 479)

Although the four-dimensional state often occurs spontaneously, certain structured situations, such as prayer, meditation or therapy, can facilitate it. In favourable circumstances these situations are characterised by stillness, silence and intense mutuality. When the four-dimensional state occurs in the one-to-one therapeutic setting it carries the conviction that healing is taking place. This is difficult to validate, because it may seem that nothing whatever is taking place, and indeed this 'nothing' may well be its prime quality. Thus a patient might remark later that a given episode was profoundly significant, when the therapist had hardly been aware of it at the time, or had completely forgotten.

Freud intuitively reached towards four dimensionality when he advocated that the patient let his associations run freely while the therapist maintains an 'evenly hovering attention'. In practice free association is extremely difficult to sustain. Most patients, however ready to oblige, find it impossible to carry out for any length of time an *instruction to be free*. The inner freedom required for free association can develop on the basis of a deep mutual trust, but this takes time. Like dreams, free association gives access to the unconscious, but having gained access, Freud thereafter chose to see *into* the unconscious rather than see *with* it; to master it rather than risk following where it might lead.

It can lead to a peculiar kind of intimacy, which Kuras called the 'intimacy of the impersonal' (1992: 433). One clinical difficulty here is that the intensity of the experience is so powerful that either patient or therapist will be inclined to abort it: the therapist by treating it as a pathological or unprofessional interaction; the patient through a deep fear of loss of self. I recall one patient who, if this particular mood began to pervade the session, would abruptly sit up, saying: 'This is getting too cosy.' The word 'cosy'

proved to be a euphemism for an alarming fear of depersonalisation. This was accompanied by fantasies of flying off the couch,
performing some strange loop-the-loop, and disappearing for
ever. In other patients it may revive fleeting memories of a blissful
mother–baby intimacy which, all too often, was abruptly ended by
being put back in the cot. The unconscious memory of this loss,
repeated again and again in infancy, leaves a lifelong fear of the
same disappointment, and a chronic avoidance of closeness and
trust.

It might be objected that what I am describing as four dimensional is no more than the time-honoured currency of the
therapeutic interaction which has always relied on empathy,
imagination and intuition, and to call it four dimensional is to
introduce unnecessarily metaphysical notions into a perfectly
familiar process. Indeed, it has always been there, just as gravity
existed before Newton drew attention to it, but to name it and
identify its singular qualities serves to enhance its efficacy. While I
am reluctant to draw a firm boundary between three- and four-
dimensional experience, in so far as imagination and symbolisation bridge them both, I would insist that it is important to clarify
the essential differences between them. Nor am I suggesting that
this kind of mutuality requires the therapist to make personal
disclosures or engage in physical contact. What I argue for is the
recognition that four dimensionality exists, that we are encompassed by it as the fish is encompassed by the sea, and that the
change of perspective brought about by our awakening to it not
only alters our view of life, but enables us to enlist its healing
power.

Repeatedly in my own clinical work, and judging from
accounts of trainees in supervision, there comes a moment – in
fact, repeated moments – of transition from disconnectedness to
connection. It may be sudden and intense or no more than a subtle
shift of feeling, but it is nonetheless crucial. In the selfsame
moment that the patient has connected with me they have
connected with themselves and I with myself: a totally new *Gestalt*
has come into being where separateness and togetherness are
simultaneously experienced in all their depth and richness. If I
insist on calling it four dimensional it is to acknowledge a
relationship beyond the therapeutic alliance, beyond the depressive position, beyond object relationship, beyond secondary
process into something which incorporates, underlies and trans-

cends the ego. Strachey persuasively argued for the mutative effect of transference interpretation (Strachey 1959: 127–159); I wish to complement this with the therapeutic effect of repeated moments of intense encounter, both positive and negative. Bit by bit the change comes to pervade the ongoing relationship and over time has a transformative effect on both parties. But where a patient comes with serious psychological damage the capacity for this type of connection may take years to reach, as illustrated in the following case.

ANALYSIS INTERMINABLE?

Mrs H. was originally referred to me simply on the grounds that she was in a marriage she desperately wanted to get out of. Given the fact that she did a demanding job, had a network of close friends and had never had a breakdown I assumed that her symptoms amounted to nothing worse than a mild obsessional neurosis. For a woman still in her twenties she looked oddly staid, with large horn rimmed glasses, thick woollen stockings, and her hair worn in a tight bun. She described her father as 'very difficult' and I had my own sense of him as an insecure, touchy but accessible sort of man. But of her mother, who she said was kind and understanding, I could somehow never form a mental image.

For the next two years she came twice a week, lay on my couch, and talked about her marital unhappiness. I couldn't form an image of her husband either, nor did I really understand why she was so desperate to leave a thoroughly decent man. She seemingly accepted most of my carefully thought-out interpretations. Our relationship was neither close nor distant. Sometimes I wondered if something was missing, that perhaps our therapeutic alliance resembled a passionless, arranged marriage, rather like the one she was already in. But since it conformed to the correct analytic attitude of benevolent neutrality, I simply got on with the job of listening and interpreting.

It was only later that she was able to tell me that she had experienced this first phase as one long torment; that she had hated coming, and only soldiered on out of blind stubbornness. She said she had been deeply afraid of me, and especially of the interminable silences I imposed. My interpretations had seemed so strange that hardly one of them made the slightest sense. I heard all this with amazement. I had seen myself as benign and facilitating; and so far from imposing long silences I felt I was inclined to say more than necessary. Her remarks revealed how far I had been from recognising the level at which her mind actually functioned. As she explained later, until coming into therapy she had felt, apart from her marriage, relatively untroubled, in that she held clear, unquestioned convictions about everything. By now I was beginning to realise that her neurotic symptoms had success-fully masked a much deeper disturbance, possibly a paranoid-schizoid condition. Although she said my interpretations made no sense, they nonetheless profoundly upset the rigid, two-dimen-sional structure by which she had always functioned.

The second phase seems linked with the actual ending of her marriage and the beginning of a period where she lived alone. By this time she had given up the couch and sat in the chair facing me. She would describe, for example, how difficult it felt to go to a party without a partner. To which I might respond:

'I think you are telling me how isolated you can feel in these situations.'

'No, I wouldn't call it isolation exactly. I sometimes have a real feeling of independence.'

'Are you saying that, up to a point, you can cope with loneliness?'

'Well, not quite. Sometimes I do feel very lonely, but not iso-lated. . . . '

'Is that because you still have good friends around you? But you seem to miss having a man of your own?'

'I value my friends enormously. They've been marvellous.'

'But you seem to be saying it doesn't quite make up for being alone?'

'No, I'm not saying that exactly. But they are mostly married, or in partnerships, and I'm not. It makes me feel. . . . '

'Different? . . . '

'No, I'm the same person.'

'I mean compared with them.'

'Well, not quite. You can be married and very lonely. I should know. . . . Oh, God, how can I explain? . . .

So it went on. Each one of my attempted clarifications missed the mark. I felt we were both caught in a desperate struggle to achieve some sort of understanding but the harder we tried the more confused we became, and invariably we would reach a state of intense reciprocal agitation. We were like a pair of mis-matched partners in a three-legged race frantically trying to get into step. I knew she was telling me something as simple as two and two making four, and I would agree that this was the case, two and two did make four, but she couldn't believe I knew what she meant and in my determination to prove that I did, the fact of two and two making four became progressively meaningless. We would reach a stage where I felt myself becoming more than a little crazy and then, at a certain moment, I would just give up. It was only when we both reached this point that something clicked and our minds suddenly synchronised. I might say:

'Then you mean . . . [whatever]?'
'That's it, *exactly*!'

We would sit back, exhausted but mutually triumphant, with a sense that at last we had made it. I noticed that at this point Mrs H. would involuntarily remove the comb from her bun and let her hair tumble down her shoulders, looking at me with a gratified smile. This same agonised struggle was repeated at nearly every session over the next year. A desperate effort to communicate which invariably ended in defeat – and then this unexpected breakthrough! Over this period she replaced her glasses with contact lenses, her woollen stockings for nylon, and let her hair hang loose. Slowly it dawned on me that she was really an attractive young woman.

The more I reflected on the maddening effect she had on me the more I realised that she had needed me to repeatedly reach this half-crazy state, because that was how she felt most of the time. I recalled my old bafflement that I couldn't form a mental image of her mother, and came to the conclusion that Mrs H. had always been mentally absorbed in her mother and therefore had no more sense of her separate existence than a fish has of the sea it swims in. In this sense their relationship had been 'too good'; metaphori-cally my patient had never left the amniotic sac. On the face of it she had struggled hard to get me to understand her, and I had responded to the limit of my ability, but at a deeper level she needed me *not* to understand her, to be 'other' to her – over against her, as her 'difficult' father had been – so that she could be 'other' to me. This long phase of paralysing non-comprehension was a good example of Winnicott's idea of the 'use of an object' (Winnicott 1971). Repeatedly she had 'destroyed' me in the sense that she paralysed my therapeutic capacity – but repeatedly, *by giving up but carrying on,* I had survived – so that she could do it all over again! 'In the end,' says Winnicott, 'we succeed by failing – failing the patient's way.'

The next phase began when she talked about ending the therapy. After all these years it seemed perfectly reasonable. But on closer questioning she confessed to a fear that she was getting ever more deeply involved with me and it frightened her. I now recalled how, when we 'clicked', she would invariably let her hair down and I noticed how satisfied she looked. This evoked in my mind the somewhat crude metaphor that, in my struggles to reach a mutual understanding, it was as if I had been engaged in a heroic battle to give a frigid woman an orgasm. Even stranger was the fact that she got one only at the moment when I admitted my impotence. It was as if being consciously understood by me, allowing her mind to be penetrated, felt like a rape. Although she wanted desperately to be understood she could only let it happen on her terms. I recalled one occasion early in the therapy when I had offered her an interpretation that, for once, immediately made sense. She flushed and said angrily:

'Why didn't I think of that?'
'Must you do everything for yourself?'
'I hate it when you're cleverer than me.'
'Is that why you never wanted a baby?'
'What do you mean?'
'Because you couldn't give *yourself* one. Because you needed a man
    to do it?'
'I'm hardly in competition with the Virgin Mary.'
'But perhaps you're in competition with me?'

The topic did not come up again, but presumably it was the occasional exchange of this kind that in the early days had made her dread therapy. I had, in that period, been vaguely aware that certain movements or postures she made on the couch seemed to me seductive. Since she had never volunteered anything about her sexual life I raised the question as delicately as I could. She assured me she had no problems in that area. I tried to explore her involvement with her father and the possibility that perhaps some of their passionate arguments disguised another sort of passion. She agreed that she might well be denying such feelings but she had no access to them. I further suggested that they may have been revived in the therapy. She looked blank, and repeated it was possible but had never occurred to her. I got no further, and although I came back to the Oedipal issue on various occasions it went nowhere. In the face of her incomprehension, I began to sound as if I was brainwashing her into an admission of erotic feelings for me, so I dropped the matter.

But when, after six years of therapy, she spoke of becoming overinvolved with me, I took up again the missing Oedipal transference: was *that* what she was afraid of? She replied: 'The way I'm involved with you is far deeper, far more exciting and frightening than sex.'

Her reply chastened me, but I decided to take a firm stand against her stopping. 'In that case, you've got no option. You're too far down the tunnel to back up; you'll just have to push through to the other end.' I think my metaphor of the tunnel unwittingly accepted that she had a deeper grasp than I of the process we were involved in, namely that this was no longer an Oedipal issue but about her struggle to be born. The fact that she was now genuinely in love with a man of her own age satisfied me that the Oedipal relationship between us had done its work, even though unconscious and unacknowledged.

Mrs H. remarried, this time with a genuine commitment; a new life began for her and in the next few years she produced two children. But our struggles were not over. The next phase of the therapy was signalled by each session opening with a silence. Beginning with five minutes, they progressively stretched to half an hour. For some reason I found them very difficult to bear. As each hour crawled by I would obsessively search for the least intrusive form of enquiry, but whatever I offered never felt right. I recalled how crazy I used to get trying to understand what she was actually telling me; now I had the even more maddening task of guessing what she might be silently thinking. After months of this, I gave up and sat in resigned silence. Then one day she said: 'This is the only place I can come where I don't have to talk.' This simple remark released me from my misery. With hindsight I realise I had been unconsciously responding to her massive but denied anxiety about mental impotence, which she had slowly worked through. I could now leave her in peace to continue with her own mysterious process. I think it was the same process as before: she had to give birth to herself, with me in attendance but without my interference.The silences became ever longer and filled the entire hour. She would come in without a word and sit down; very soon her eyelids would flicker, then close; whereupon I felt free to shut my own and let my thoughts drift where they would. From time to time I might glance across to where she sat; occasionally her eyes would open onto vacancy, then close again as she slipped back into her strange, trance-like state, somewhere between sleep and waking. It was unbelievably peaceful, although I sometimes found it difficult to resist the idea that the whole thing was absurd. Yet the hour seemed to pass all too quickly and Mrs H. would leave with a heartfelt: 'Thank you.' Gradually the silences shortened again: she would 'wake' with a warm smile, as if to say 'Oh, hello – you're there!' and then begin: 'I've been thinking...' What followed was an interchange as alive and clear as our previous struggles had been fraught and incomprehensible. Eventually I invited her to describe what happened in her silences. She replied:

They vary. Sometimes I'm muddled, which is my normal condition. I can't get away from my thoughts. But at their best, which is now very often, they're marvellous. It's as if all the confusion in my mind settles and I begin to see. Just *see*. You, for example. The fact is for years I never saw you. Then, at a certain moment, my eyes really opened and I saw you.

She hesitated, then looked directly into my face and said with embarrassment:

I think what I see is your soul. I seem able only to get into that state in here, in this chair. Until I can manage it outside of here, with others, I can't risk leaving. I know you think I've been coming a very long time, but I'm convinced it has had to take this long. When I first came I was completely locked into my private world; I was always tense but at the same time secure, I even thought I was happy in it. It was you who broke up that world, you who made me unhappy and insecure and I hated you for that. At least that's how I saw it. I had to resist and, inside me, fight everything you said, or I would really have had a breakdown. Or left. I don't think you understood: you were a man, and in my eyes very powerful; you knew all the answers; and if you didn't understand me, I must be the one in the wrong. You broke into my safe world. It's true you let the light in but it was blinding, and I could only take it in tiny bits. I could never really look at you. I don't think you realised that either. I can look at you now and not be blinded. Trust me. I'll know when it's time to go.

As I understood it, she was describing the long, painful transition first from a two-dimensional level of polarised certainties to a three-dimensional level of ambivalence and confusion, and thence, by means of our shared silences, to intermittent glimpses of the four-dimensional level of clear sight.

Chapter 9

The spectrum of treatment

Freud regarded psychoanalysis as the most refined of all therapeutic methods, 'pure gold' compared to the inferior 'copper' of its competitors, and few psychoanalysts would dissent from that view. Refined it may well be, but numerous research studies have not ranked it as necessarily the most successful. In fact, the psychodynamic therapies generally have fared rather badly in the surveys of therapeutic outcome (Malan 1973). But the situation is rather more complicated, in so far as most of these studies have themselves proved to be methodologically flawed and their criteria for improvement not sufficiently sophisticated. As the quality of the research has improved, analytic psychotherapy increasingly comes to look more effective. Nonetheless it has to be conceded that forms of psychotherapeutic treatment other than psychoanalysis can justifiably claim their share of good results, depending on circumstances and the nature of the disorder.

If a patient is chronically demented, violent, suicidal or liable to die from malnutrition, the need for direct medical intervention may be self-evident. Some of the older drastic interventions, such as lobotomy, relieved acute depression but only at the cost of the patient being permanently reduced to a partially vegetative condition. The surgical form of lobotomy has long fallen out of favour, but the pharmacological equivalent is still widely administered in mental hospitals. By taking large doses of emotionally anaesthetising drugs, patients suffer less but their quality of life is much reduced. Because the action of drugs is so much cruder than the marvellous precision of dosage provided by the body's own remedial powers, the benefits are diminished by the side effects. Yet it must be conceded that, given the constraints of time, money and resources, many of the more sophisticated drugs are necessary and effective. Biological factors are clearly associated with psychopathological conditions. For example, low concentrations of certain monoamine neurotransmitters in the brain can be observed in states of depression. To remedy the imbalance by modifying the body chemistry is, in the terms of the model I am proposing, to deal with the problem 'one dimensionally'. The same could be said of hypnosis, suggestion, diet, bedrest and other measures that address the mind or body directly.

Whereas drugs are prescribed for a wide range of emotional and mental disorders, phobic and obsessional states can be effectively treated by desensitisation methods. This amounts to progressively retraining behavioural reactions, such as panic in the presence of spiders, the dread of heights, enclosed spaces, physical contamination, as well as sexual dysfunction and substance abuse. The behavioural method addresses not the body but the overt symptom, and aims to break old compulsive patterns by a graduated system of positive and negative reinforcements. This is another name for the time-honoured method of reward and punishment commonly employed in prisons, schools, work situations and military training. In fact it is by far the most widely used instrument of socialisation. Since one of the most severe social punishments is shaming, behaviour modification can be used positively in group situations: hence the relative effectiveness of organisations such as 'Weight Watchers' or 'Alcoholics Anonymous' where members are both coerced and encouraged into habits of personal restraint. Alcohol addiction can also be retrained medically, for example, by prescribing substances (or even implanting them surgically) which produce nausea when alcohol enters the system. The rationale is that after a sufficient number of bad experiences a negatively toned conditioned reflex will be established that obliterates further temptation. Behavioural techniques may justifiably be regarded as a two-dimensional approach; they bring change by learning from experience, good and bad. The real test of the method comes when the group support or disapproval is no longer available; or when an acute life crisis occurs. Nevertheless behavioural treatments can justifiably claim to be the initial treatment of choice with specific disorders.

The vast sum of help provided for the mentally ill by relations and friends cannot be overestimated. For the most part it is a long-suffering, largely unpaid, provision of care, tolerance and containment. In everyday life personal care tends to take the form of sympathetic listening and simple advice giving, the supply of which fortunately always exceeds demand. Optimally, this amounts to an education in common sense – and some people actually do sometimes listen to reason. Friendly listening and helpful advice is a valuable form of person-to-person counselling which, in its more sophisticated forms, has developed into psychotherapy.

The psychotherapist, in fact, carefully avoids giving advice or trying to eliminate troublesome symptoms, but seeks to identify the reasons why they occur. A wide variety of psychotherapies, each with its specific focus, fall into this category: brief, cognitive, humanistic, *Gestalt*, transactional, existentialist, 'rational–emotive', each claiming its share of success. Psycho-analysis, with its concentrated focus on unconscious processes and its rigorous exclusion of other forms of persuasion such as education and reassurance, claims to be the most penetrating of them all, but is restricted to patients with considerable time and money and some capacity for insight. In so far as all these approaches seek to strengthen the patient's rational ego, I would term them three-dimensional.

In practice each type of therapy referred to above, in spite of its declared focus, inevitably touches at least two, if not all three, levels in the patient. The average sympathetic doctor, in addition to drugs, usually offers advice, reassurance and sometimes a listening ear. A bio-energetics practitioner who physically touches a patient will also explore their thoughts and feelings; they could claim that in the early stages of treatment of severe disorders talk is irrelevant and possibly counter-productive. The behavioural therapist cannot help but form a relationship with his client and convey that he or she matters, and this, albeit unanalysed, relationship will have a therapeutic effect. Psychotherapists, although they avoid giving advice, unavoidably educate their patients into an altogether different kind of thinking and also function as behavioural models by the way they address a given situation. Psychoanalysts go to great lengths to avoid extraneous influences: thus they sit well out of sight, carefully monitor all their natural responses, and concentrate purely on interpretation. But they are well aware that, in practice, patients use every minute clue to determine the analyst's 'true' feelings towards them – tones of voice, sighs, breathing, evidence of restlessness – and develop an uncanny sense of their analyst's genuineness. Simply by going on being there in a benevolently neutral way the analyst conveys that the patient matters. Although the analyst scrupulously avoids teaching, the patient invariably contrives to learn what is useful to him or her; for example, by recognising how much the inner life is influenced by childhood or by the unconscious.

In a broad assessment of the psychotherapeutic process, Jung differentiated four ways in which the patient used the therapy: first for *confession*, whereby the patient could be relieved of guilt and grievance. When this was accompanied by powerful emotion, it served to unburden the heart and cleanse the soul, a process Freud called abreaction. The second way Jung identified as *education*, an area which in his day Adlerian psychology made its speciality but which has since been incorporated into other approaches such as cognitive-analytical therapy. The third Jung called *elucidation*, generally known as interpretation, the method specifically developed by Freud. Jung did not dispute that both the Adlerian and Freudian methods fulfilled important therapeutic functions, especially for younger people struggling to cope with relationships, a career, and life in general. But for those who had gone beyond this, older and already established in the world, who now sought above all to find a meaning to their lives, there is a fourth approach. Jung called it *transformation*, and regarded it as uniquely his own (Jung 1954: 53ff.).

Unlike the original Adlerian and Freudian methods, where the analyst does something to or for the patient, Jung emphasised the therapist's profound involvement in the process. Ferenczi had experimented with a similar approach in the earliest days of the analytic movement whereby he would engage with his patient in 'mutual analysis', but the project came to grief. In recent years a number of psychoanalysts have independently arrived at positions much closer to the transformational effect of working *with* the patient. In the US the intense reciprocal involvement of therapist and patient has characterised the work of Harold Searles, to the extent of regarding himself as his 'patient's patient' (Searles 1975). In the UK the dedicated, innovative spirit of Ferenczi was continued by Michael Balint, his analysand and junior colleague (Balint 1968). Another major figure was Michael Fordham, whose achievement was to integrate the psychoanalytic insights of Melanie Klein with the vision of Jung (Fordham 1969). Clinically he brought to analytical psychology, which can be all too prone to defensive idealisation, the rigour and scepticism of psychoanalysis; theoretically he expanded Jung's work by demonstrating that the urge towards individuation does not simply begin in the latter half of life but occurs from the earliest years and extends throughout life. Thus Fordham's work anticipated and embodied the convergence of psychoanalysis and analytical psychology that I suggest is now taking place.

There are now many contemporary psychoanalytic practitioners who have adopted what might be called a transformational perspective, but the two who have carried psychoanalysis furthest in this direction are Winnicott and Bion (Winnicott 1971; Bion 1970). In linking their specific contributions to those of Jung, it is not my intention to conflate them or to demonstrate how they are all saying the same thing but rather to indicate how each, from their individual thought and experience, points towards the next development in psychotherapy. Nor is it my intention to cover the full range of their work but to focus on this 'new experimental paradigm' each has discovered.

Chapter 10

The area of convergence

JUNG AS HEALER

In an earlier chapter I referred to the ancient form of healing known as shamanism, and suggested that all subsequent forms of treatment, both physical and psychological, derive from it. A considerable literature now exists on shamanism, originally drawing on reports by ethnographers and explorers of primitive communities, and latterly by educated native psychiatrists and anthropologists. In all of these societies the shaman held a very special place, sometimes revered, sometimes feared, but always regarded as a unique type of individual who both belonged to, yet was apart from, the community he or she served. Although the specific healing techniques vary from society to society, even from tribe to tribe, the one ability every shaman possesses is to enter into a trance in order to make direct contact with the spirit world. There he or she encounters demons, or dead relatives, or animal spirits and, risking great dangers, tries to gain their help on the sufferer's behalf. One type of journey involves searching the nether regions for the sufferer's lost soul which had been stolen, often during sleep. Loss of soul was the most severe of the primitive illnesses; its contemporary equivalent would be a suicidal depression or a borderline schizoid state.

The shamanic gift may run in families, or certain individuals may be marked out by temperament for this particular vocation. Shamans differ from normal members of their community by having, or developing, certain deviant tendencies, such as fainting fits, hysterical episodes, visions; many shamans are of uncertain sexual identity, and some live as a 'wife' to a male partner. The majority have suffered a serious illness in early life, or develop their shamanic vocation after a life-threatening accident or illness which opens up an altered view of existence. Often the sufferer has to become a healer in order to be cured, and this involves going through a long and severe training conducted by a senior shaman. These special initiatory rites may require prolonged endurance of pain, which itself may induce altered states of consciousness. The culmination of the process is the experience of psychic death and dismemberment, ultimately leading to rebirth. The shaman is often helped by an animal spirit or a 'celestial wife', the latter a figure who parallels the 'soror mystica' of the alchemist, or the 'dakini' of tantric mysticism. A contemporary account of the shamanic initiatory process, describing incidents so startling as sometimes to defy credibility, appears in the work of Carlos Castaneda (1971).

Groesbeck (1989) has described how Jung fulfilled many of the conditions that made him eligible to become a healer. In his earliest years he suffered from eczema, had suicidal urges, and fantasies of hearing people drown, women weeping, and seeing men in black boots and coats. In his *Memories, Dreams, Reflections* (1971) Jung described how, at the age of 3 or 4, he had a terrifying dream of a tree trunk made of naked flesh sitting on a throne in an underground cave. It was surmounted by a faceless head, with a single eye at its tip gazing upwards. He recalls his mother calling out in the dream: 'Yes, just look at him. That is the man eater.' A reductive interpretation of this giant phallus, together with his mother's comment, might see it as essentially Oedipal. But it brought Jung, at this tender age, into contact with the deeper mystery of a subterranean nature god that knew nothing of the spirit, yet with an eye that could look only upwards, as if seeking the light. Groesbeck comments (1989) that images of the tree have strong connections with the central shamanic conception of the 'world tree' which supports heaven and earth.

In his early years Jung had other disturbing symptoms, fits of choking and fainting, images of people with detached heads, a general sense of alienation from his fellows, and later a startling realisation that he was 'two persons'. 'Number One' was extroverted, curious, intellectual; 'Number Two' was remote, introverted, close to nature, old and mistrustful but also mystical and intuitive (Jung 1971: 75ff.). The existence of these two distinct personalities was evidence of his capacity to dissociate. As Eliade observes, dissociation is essential to shamanic experience (1964).

Dissociation or splitting is by no means uncommon. Indeed psychoanalysis sees it as a universal tendency, and if some measure of re-integration does not take place, illness manifests. But it may also be the source of direct, psychic knowledge, and it gave Jung the gift of seeing things in telepathic and visionary ways. His capacity to understand dreams was quite uncanny: from the dream alone he could differentiate a physical from a psychic illness. The dissociative tendency can be a curse or a blessing, and many of my own hysterically inclined patients have shown evidence of psychic gifts, a phenomenon also noted by Balint (1958).

In so far as Jung was able to assimilate his dissociative and pathological tendencies it places him, like the shaman, in the category of the 'wounded healer'; or more precisely, one who heals by virtue of the *partial* healing of his own wound, since if it had healed completely he might too easily forget how it felt to be sick and his capacity to identify with the patient would be impaired. In Greek mythology the original wounded healer was the legendary founder of medicine, the centaur Chiron, who suffered an incurable wound and whose pain could never cease because, as a demi-god, he could never die.

In his student days Jung was fascinated by his cousin Helene, who was both a medium and a hysteric, and he even based his medical dissertation on the psychic phenomena which he encountered in her (Jung 1957). At least two other women in his life, Sabina Spielrein and Toni Wolf, were also known to have functioned as 'celestial wives'; that is to say, he was both sexually and spiritually drawn to them, but also received from them considerable knowledge and wisdom. Throughout his mature years Jung was surrounded by a number of devoted women, ironically labelled the 'Jungfrau', many of whom were creative, intelligent and spiritually minded.

Jung conformed to the general type of shamanic healer; he was subject to archetypal dreams and prophetic visions, in which specific individuals from the 'other world' acted as helping spirits and guides. In practical terms, Jung developed his visionary capacity into the technique of 'active imagination'. In clinical practice this involves, for example, inviting the patient to fantasise from the point where a dream leaves off and to 'dream the dream onwards'. Not every patient can use this technique, but when it works it produces a singularly creative and healing experience.

Jung seemed able, like the shaman, to induce the dissociative capacity in himself by 'lowering his consciousness'; this gave him greater access to the patient's unconscious and a direct sense of what it felt like to be the other person. When this state of mutual fusion takes place, the patient too must have a sense of profound connection, bringing the healing awareness that, for a little while, his unbearable isolation has ceased. Jung placed a high value on these phases of inner connection which culminated in the 'coniunctio' (1954: 165ff.), a term borrowed from alchemy.

A glimpse of Jung at work may be found in his account of a young patient, brought up in the East, who underwent the most bizarre physical symptoms during her analysis (1954: 333–5). The treatment had 'got stuck in the doldrums'. Then Jung had a dream in which the patient appeared on a balcony high above him, bathed in a golden light, as if she were a goddess. Jung chose to tell the patient his dream, whereupon:

> her real neurosis began, and it left me completely flabbergasted. It started with a series of highly impressive dreams, which I could not understand at all, and then she developed symptoms whose cause, structure and significance were absolutely incomprehensible to me. They first took the form of an indefinable excitation in the perineal region, and she dreamt that a white elephant was coming out of her genitals. She was so impressed by this she tried to carve the elephant out of ivory.... Soon afterwards symptoms of uterine ulcers appeared, and I had to send the patient to a gynaecologist.... Suddenly this symptom disappeared, and she developed a severe hyperaesthesia of the bladder. She had to leave the room two or three times during the consulting hour. No local infection could be found. Psychologically, the symptom meant that something had to be 'ex-pressed'. So I gave her the task of expressing by drawings whatever her hand suggested to her. She had never drawn before, and set about it with much doubt and hesitation. But now symmetrical flowers took shape under her hand, vividly coloured and arranged in symbolic patterns....
> Meanwhile the hyperaesthesia of the bladder had ceased, but intestinal spasms developed higher up, causing gurgling noises and sounds of splashing that could be heard even outside the room.... These symptoms gradually abated after

several weeks. Their place was then taken by a strange paraesthesia of the head. The patient had the feeling that the top of her skull was growing soft, that the fontanelle was opening up, and that a bird with a long sharp beak was coming down to pierce through the fontanelle as far as the diaphragm.

Jung reports how these symptoms left him completely baffled, whereas the patient felt it was all 'going splendidly'. Then he came across an account of Tantric Yoga describing the seven chakras, each represented by a lotus flower, and this explained all the things he had not understood.

The nethermost chakra, called muladhara, is the perineal lotus and corresponds to the cloacal zone in Freud's sexual theory. This centre, like all the others, is represented in the shape of a flower.... The next chakra, called svadhistahana, is localised near the bladder and represents the sexual centre... the perineal chakra contains as its main symbol the sacred white elephant.

Jung proceeds to plot the course of his patient's physical disturbances as they ascended her body, chakra by chakra, culminating in a fantasy of the piercing of the crown of the head. From the evidence it would appear that she had undergone, quite spontaneously, the rare event of the rising of the kundalini. At this point the patient gave up the treatment and confessed that she did not want an overwhelming psychic experience but a real, live baby. It seemed a rather mundane conclusion to a fascinating process, but clearly the young patient was not prepared to follow a path of life totally alien to her expectations. Jung comments:

Although this case is an unusual one, it is not an exception. It has served its purpose if it has enabled me to give you some idea of my psychotherapeutic procedure. The case is not in the least a story of triumph; it is more like a saga of blunders, hesitations, doubts, gropings in the dark, and false clues which in the end took a favourable turn. But all this comes very much nearer the truth and reality of my procedure than a case that brilliantly confirms the preconceived opinions and intentions of the therapist.

(Jung 1954)

The alchemical model of the transference–countertransference experience was one of Jung's most original and fertile discoveries. He devoted years of research into the alchemical tradition of Europe in the Middle Ages, unearthing with scholarly thoroughness a vast area of spiritual endeavour that had fallen into neglect, and linking it with modern psychotherapy (Jung 1944). In doing so he provided a link with the alchemical tradition that had long before reached a highly sophisticated form in ancient China; the equally ancient tantric mystical tradition of India, and even going back to the shamanic healing practices of the primitive world.

He was familiar with the implications of modern scientific developments, including Relativity Theory, and connected it with his own therapeutic capacities. 'Since intuition seems to function as if there were no space, and sometimes as if there were no time, you might say that I add a fourth dimension' (Jung 1944). He was able to develop his knowledge of modern science through personal contact with one of the leading physicists of the time, Wolfgang Pauli, who had become his patient and later collaborated with him in developing his theory of synchronicity. Synchronous events occur when events in the outer world uncannily parallel those in the inner world: that is, they are meaningful coincidences that suggest a unity of existence where subjectivity and objective reality interweave. In a like manner Jung regarded physics and psychology as two aspects of the same unknown reality.

In the mainstream of psychoanalytic debate Jung's ideas, indeed his very existence, are little mentioned. This may be the legacy of the rupture that took place between Freud and Jung over seventy years ago. It was more than a clash of personalities: each took a fundamentally different stance towards 'nature' or the unconscious. Jung's inclination was to learn from it and Freud's to control it. Freud saw the unconscious as a blind, impersonal force, manifested in the ruthlessly pleasure-seeking id. Jung, by contrast, regarded the human unconscious as part of a collective unconscious which was as vast, mysterious and creative as nature itself. Freud regarded Jung's 'occult' ideas as a betrayal of all his highest scientific aspirations. The irony is that, with the passage of time, a great many of Jung's original ideas and observations are now being supported by scientific research and rediscovered by psychoanalysis. Kohut's celebrated 'psychology of the self' is a case in point (Kohut 1977). Discussion of the centrality of the self has been the staple of Jungian discourse for half a century but

Kohut appears to have discovered it quite independently. The psychoanalyst Arnold Modell, in his recent book *The Private Self* (1993), arrived at essentially Jungian ideas concerning the impact of 'values' on the psyche eighty years after Jung, and with hardly an acknowledgement. But it needs to be recognised that in the history of thought old formulations resurface 'in a new context, a new language, through new experiences, and with newly discerned implications' (Tresan 1996), so that no one, Jung and Freud included, can claim the exclusive patent on a given idea.

WINNICOTT: CLOSE ENCOUNTERS IN TRANSITIONAL SPACE

One of the psychoanalysts who did acknowledge Jung's originality was Winnicott. Prior to his analytic training Winnicott had practised as a paediatrician. He was gifted with a special empathy for the minds of small children and this enabled him to bring a new vision to psychoanalysis, often expressed in arrestingly simple yet paradoxical insights. Where Freud and Klein were concerned with drives and the struggle for mastery over them, Winnicott saw the healthy infant as steeped in creativity. While he did not, like Ferenczi, directly challenge Freud's 'rule of abstinence' he chose to regard it as a necessary but later phase of the therapeutic process. He subscribed to the idea that the severely damaged patient needed first an experience of benign illusion, similar to that provided by 'an ordinary devoted mother' to her newborn infant. Thanks to her state of 'primary maternal preoccupation' a healthy mother is able to offer her child not just a totally dependable environment but a hyper-sensitivity to its inarticulate needs. By meeting the 'gesture of its omnipotence' she makes it possible for her infant to lay down the basis of a self it can increasingly call its own. Winnicott envisaged the 'infinitely subtle' communications between a mother and her baby working like this:

> The baby says (wordlessly of course): 'I just feel like . . . ' and just then the mother comes along and turns the baby over, or she comes with the feeding apparatus and the baby becomes able to finish the sentence: ' . . . a turn-over, a breast, nipple, milk, etc., etc.' We have to say the baby created the breast, but could not have done so had not the mother come along with the breast just

at that moment. The communication to the baby is 'Come at the world creatively, create the world; it is only what you create that has meaning for you.'

Next comes: 'the world is in your control'. From this initial experience of omnipotence the baby is able to begin to experience frustration and even to arrive one day at the other extreme from omnipotence, that is to say, having a sense of being a mere speck in the universe. . . . Is it not from being God that human beings arrive at the humility proper to human individuality?

(Winnicott 1988)

As Winnicott makes clear, the state of omnipotence is an absolutely necessary illusion but from a certain stage of development it is equally necessary that the mother fail her infant and set in train a graduated process of disillusion:

Human beings fail and fail, and in the course of ordinary care a mother is all the time mending her failures. These relative failures with immediate remedy undoubtedly add up eventually to a communication, so that the baby comes to know about success.

(Winnicott 1988)

In summing up Winnicott's views of the illusion–disillusion process, Sue Norrington remarks: 'paradoxically it is the relative failures which give a baby a sense of proper disillusion, so long as he has been able to experience proper omnipotence and illusion' (Norrington 1993: 10).

Winnicott's most celebrated discovery is the concept of the 'transitional object' which he saw as occupying a 'third area' that exists between inner and outer reality. It may be a teddy bear or a piece of blanket that the infant becomes attached to, but it serves as both an extension of itself yet something other than itself. He regarded the relationship to the transitional object as the beginning of the sense of meaning in life, the source of one's 'true self', and later as the foundation of art and creative endeavour of every kind. He said:

I am drawing attention to the paradox involved in the use by the infant of what I have called the transitional object. My contribution is to ask for a paradox to be accepted and tolerated and respected, and for it not to be resolved.

(Winnicott 1971: xii)

Winnicott's true self is a paradoxical idea that everyone feels they recognise but none can adequately describe. It echoes the ancient idea of the soul yet is intimately involved with the body. Our true selves can connect at the deepest level but are ultimately unreachable. 'Although healthy persons communicate and enjoy communicating, the other fact is equally true, that each individual is an isolate, permanently non-communicating, permanently unknown, in fact unfound' (Winnicott 1964). It may be characterised by the spontaneous act devoid of calculation, a look or gesture without the least trace of self-consciousness. In its creative aspect, it happens when we stop trying to grasp an idea but open ourselves to it; it happens when the novelist finds the characters of his book writing their own dialogue; or when the athlete no longer has to force himself to run because the running has taken over; these are the effortless phases in life when it all works as if 'by magic'.

Closely connected with the true self is the idea of spontaneous play. It was Winnicott who first had the temerity to introduce into the serious business of psychotherapy the idea of play.

Psychotherapy takes place in the overlap of two areas of playing, that of the patient and that of the therapist. Psychotherapy has to do with two people playing together. The corollary of this is that where playing is not possible then the work done by the therapist is directed towards bringing the patient from a state of not being able to play into a state of being able to play.

(Winnicott 1971: 63)

Here I envisage him to include the play of ideas, the play of feeling, the play of intuition and imagination, so that patient and therapist will, at their best, be like two instrumentalists engaged in a creative improvisation. While it is not identical with Jung's 'active imagination' it operates in the same area of the mind. Living creatively is what Winnicott seems always to be aiming for, and it takes place in what he calls 'potential space'. The equivalent space in Jungian terminology is the 'pleroma'. Just as Jung could say that 'the only events in my life worth telling are those where the imperishable world irrupted into this transitory one' (Jung 1971: 18), so Winnicott regarded transitional or potential space as 'the place where we live' (Winnicott 1974: 122ff.).

While claiming an allegiance to both Freud and Melanie Klein, his position is profoundly divergent from theirs. For Freud, good behaviour arises from the guilt for crimes, usually of an Oedipal nature, committed in phantasy against one parent or the other. For Klein love is a form of reparation for damage inflicted on the mother. It is as if 'We need to be good to make up for being bad' (Eigen 1981: 418). Both Freud and Klein subscribed to the notion of a fundamentally ruthless life force that only becomes modified under the pressure of survival. Thus the baby's smile is not simply one of joyful recognition but is intended to evoke a mothering response; essentially the infant seduces and manipulates. The Freud–Klein account of development is that it proceeds by way of projection and introjection, which involves the constant splitting, adaptation and manipulation of the ego in order to achieve mastery of the id and of external reality. In his earlier paper on the development of the capacity for concern, Winnicott subscribed to the Kleinian view that concern arose out of guilt, but later, in 'The use of an object' (1971) he shifted to a radically different viewpoint. While Winnicott recognises destructive attacks by the infant on its mother, he does not see these as necessarily hostile. They simply express the natural aggressive force of life, like a chicken breaking out of its shell. In Winnicott's terms the infant repeatedly 'destroys' the mother in order to find that she survives. In essence it is a creative act, since in the act of destruction and separation both subject and object take on a new reality for each other.

> The subject says to the object: 'I destroyed you', and the object is there to receive the communication. From now on the subject says: 'Hullo object!' 'I destroyed you.' 'I love you.' 'You have value for me because of your survival of my destruction of you.' 'While I am loving you I am all the time destroying you in (unconscious) fantasy.'
>
> (Winnicott 1971)

Eigen comments:

> A quantum leap is in progress ... wherein self and the other are freshly created through one another.... In contrast the Freudian

reality basically requires some degree of depersonalization for adaptation and mastery to become possible.... All that exists of importance is the fact that we are real together, living in the amazing sense of becoming more and more real, where destructiveness makes love real, and love makes destructiveness creative.

(Eigen 1981: 416)

It is in his later ideas on the creative aspect of destruction that Winnicott links with Jung's notion of transformation and Fordham's of 'de-integration', regarding it as inherent in the whole developmental process from the earliest stages of life. 'What is good,' Winnicott said, 'is always being destroyed.' When asked why this should be so, he replied: 'Because it's necessary.'

BION'S FAITH

Although the work of Jung and Winnicott takes full account of a larger dimension, Bion's thought appears to be the most radical in that the concept he termed 'O' goes beyond all notions of dimensionality. He wrote:

I shall use the sign 'O' to denote that which is ultimate reality, absolute truth, the godhead, the infinite, the thing-in-itself. O does not fall in the domain of knowledge or learning save incidentally: it can 'become', but it cannot be 'known'.

(Bion 1970: 26)

In positing this hypothetical 'O' as ultimate reality Bion aligns himself with the tradition of metaphysical and idealist philosophers, most notably Plato and Kant, a tradition which continues in David Bohm's concept of an implicate order. The particular 'absolute' which Bion most values is the goal that science aspires to: namely truth. Even though it can never be reached, the ceaseless pursuit of the truth is the prime condition of a meaningful life. Whereas truth's opposite, the lie, is the source of all sickness. What Bion enjoins upon us is paradoxical: in searching for the truth we search for something we know can never be found but without which life lacks meaning.

In his view this same search applies in every analytic session. He urges the analyst to seek only the 'O' of the session, the 'O' of the patient; that is, the patient's spirit, essence, 'true self'. Do we achieve this by knowing more and more *about* the patient, or does that inhibit the possibility of really *knowing* him or her directly? Bion says cryptically; 'One cannot know O, one must be it' (1970: 27). There is a profound difference between knowing and being; they occupy different existential dimensions. Yet they are inextricably entwined. Simply knowing about ourselves or another does not really help us become who we are.

The single-minded search for 'O' has far-reaching implications for the analytic method. This Bion says, in his now familiar phrase, must be conducted without memory, desire, or understanding. These are the forms of knowing which impede being. Even the desire to heal or help may also work against becoming 'O' in that they do not accept the present reality but seek to change it. 'O' is 'darkness and formlessness', Bion says. Here we are reminded of the transformations of the imaginal couple engaged in the alchemical process: two of the stages they pass through are *nigredo* and *massa confusa*. Likewise where Jung speaks of the transformative potential of the coniunctio, Bion speaks of 'at-one-ment'.

Traditional analysis is based on the changes brought about by understanding how we each came to be as we are. Thus the analyst learns all he or she can about the patient's past and present life, in order to link them and make sense of them for the patient; or, better still, help the patient make sense of them for him or herself. Undoubtedly, with increased understanding comes some release from confusion, panic, guilt, blind hatred – from the torments of psychopathological states. But too great an eagerness to help, know and understand may actually impede the glimpses of emotional truth the session might offer: the analytic space becomes 'saturated' and inimical to 'O'. Freud too warned against what he called the *furor sanandi*, the rage to heal.

It is also the therapist's acknowledged task to act as an emotional 'container' for the patient. Thus if a patient generates an atmosphere of hysteria, it is no part of the analyst's role to become infected by it, but rather to contain it. This involves some capacity to think, a task, as Bion has emphasised, comparable to that of the mother who absorbs and detoxifies her baby's primitive dreads by virtue of her capacity for reverie.

But for the analyst to be merely sane is to leave the patient drowning in his private horrors while the analyst stays safely on dry land. Even if you throw a rope to a drowning man, it's of no help if he can't take hold of it. In certain situations it may be necessary to jump overboard and go to where he happens to be, even though the therapist takes the risk of drowning too. In practice this means that, when a patient is in such a panic he or she cannot even listen, it may be necessary to abandon the defences that separate the therapist and patient, to go down into the patient's desperation, and consciously share it. To do this requires the courage that only faith can give, since it involves the therapist in a partial identification with the patient's condition. Bion says: 'Any attempt to cling to what he [the analyst] knows must be resisted for the sake of achieving a state of mind analogous to the schizoid-paranoid position' (Bion 1970).

I think what he is suggesting is that the analyst allow him or herself to enter into a voluntary and partial breakdown in order that a new insight may break through. This is a prescription so radical that it is not surprising that many analysts cannot take it seriously, and that Bion himself adhered rigorously to the classical technique. Yet his mystical perspective is at an even further remove than Winnicott's from the logical-positivist framework of Freud, whose originality Bion deeply respected. In a like manner Bion presents, by means of neo-mathematical formulae and in language of baffling precision, ideas of the utmost para-doxicality, even more idiosyncratic than those of Winnicott. The effect of reading Bion is much the same as wrestling with a Zen 'koan'; one's familiar frame of reference disintegrates, there is a sense of becoming somewhat crazy with incomprehension, but in recovering from the state of breakdown that he induces we may find we have broken through into a new level of understanding.

TOWARDS A NEW PARADIGM

Where do Jung, Winnicott and Bion converge and how do they diverge from orthodox analysis? Classical analysis is charac-terised by certain basic assumptions: it assumes a healthy therapist who is helping a sick patient to get better. It aims at strengthening the ego and making the unconscious conscious. It values clarity, knowledge, insight, and understanding. It relies heavily on speech. It is uneasy with regression and mistrusts the primitive. It abhors error. It is deeply concerned with the past.

By contrast Jung, as we have seen, emphasised the mutual involvement of therapist and patient, and the possibility that they might heal each other; indeed, he assumed that if the therapist cannot change, neither can the patient. From this it follows that the therapist need no longer be the only one who has all the answers, but can learn from the patient in a shared journey of discovery. In Jung we find, in addition to a rational understanding of the unconscious, a readiness to learn from it and co-operate with it. This same spirit is both implicit and explicit in Winnicott, where we noted that the therapist is not only engaged in the serious business of healing but can also be allowed to play; especially if the therapist can help the patient learn how to play, and in fact the two are not mutually exclusive. Jung encouraged his patients freely to paint, sculpt and even dance in order to express their innermost selves. Melanie Klein's most original discoveries came out of enabling her child patients to play, but her adult patients were restricted to words, especially to a chastening recognition of their destructive tendencies. Nonetheless the post-Kleinian approach, like the Jungian, is essentially a mythological/religious one. In the words of one leading post-Kleinian writer:

> Every person has to have what you might describe as a 'religion' in which his internal objects perform the function of Gods – but it is not a religion that derives its power because of belief in these Gods but because these Gods do in fact perform functions in the mind. Therefore if you do not put your trust in them you are in trouble, and this trouble is the trouble of narcissism.
>
> (Meltzer 1981)

Winnicott valued not only the clarity of meaningful interpretation but the mystery of paradox; he recognised that in paradox the truly mutative truths are enfolded. The therapist is no longer required to present him or herself to the patient as a blank screen or a well polished mirror but to be, as far as possible, his or her centred, natural, spontaneous self; a model Jung deeply subscribed to. And since it is human to err, this also includes the possibility of error. In Winnicott's view a therapist is expected not only to succeed, he or she must also be allowed to fail – 'to fail in the patient's way' – providing he or she can recover. What Winnicott aims at is not necessarily more happiness, or even freedom from symptoms, but more spontaneous life, even if it involves risk and suffering. Winnicott's 'true self', like Jung's 'archetype of the self', goes beyond Freud's ego with its laudable goals of love and work, and occupies a different existential dimension.

Even more mystical is Bion's unknowable 'O' which he tells us is what every analytic session must aim at. Like Jung's individuation, Bion's truth can never be reached or indeed known. And since it is unknowable the therapist must learn to be an expert in 'unknowing'; in having no truths to hold onto beyond an unshakeable dedication to truth itself. The therapist endlessly wonders about the mystery that is the patient; if he or she can inspire in the patient a sense of wonder about him or herself, then both may become 'wonderful' and the therapy is on course.

Bion's theory of thinking involves the extraordinary assumption that thoughts exist prior to a thinker. In the small infant these 'proto-thoughts' are little more than sense data; they pre-exist thought proper which involves the capacity for symbolisation, but have the power to affect how we structure our experience. Bion called them pre-conceptions: only when a pre-conception mates with a realisation can development occur. In Jung's terms it would be described as an archetypal expectation of parenting encountering a real parent. From the positive realisation, such as the breast being available when the child desires it, comes the sense of agency; what Winnicott described as meeting the child's gesture of omnipotence. From the negative realisation, when the breast fails to materialise, there comes a breakdown which offers the possibility of a leap to a new level of development, namely, the capacity for thought. This breakdown–breakthrough process, which attends all development, Bion called 'catastrophic change'.

Given the dreadful contingencies of human life, the omnipresence of suffering, the lifelong struggle for survival, the appalling ruthlessness and self-deception inherent in human nature, it is difficult to deny the deep scepticism that informs Freud's vision. Yet to regard the capacity for joy as always a derived form of something else, to deduce that love, wholeness, goodness are no more than defensive compensations, is to throw out baby with the bath water. It is based on the assumption that reality stops at the three dimensional and anything beyond that is a delusion; that the conviction of at-one-ment that attends the four-dimensional state is really a regressive state of fusion which we knew in infancy, a futile and imaginary longing for a lost paradise.

Yet the four dimensional, to which Jung, Winnicott and Bion each in their different ways subscribed, does in fact exist. It is not imaginary but imaginal. It is not a delusion, but carries with it the subjective conviction of being our true state; or at least closer to our true state than everyday consciousness. In this sense the four dimensional is closer to us than we are to ourselves, since it is life itself. 'By life,' D.H. Lawrence said, 'we mean something that gleams, that has the four-dimensional quality.' Viewed from the three-dimensional perspective it appears to be an altered state, but from the four-dimensional viewpoint everyday consciousness is itself an altered state, a shrunken, blemished condition that leaves us suffering from a chronic sense of insufficiency. It is undeniable that a great many lives are damaged by the failure and abuse that occurs in childhood; but clinical practice demonstrates that just as often it is the denial of our creative, emotional and spiritual potential that drives people into misery, neurosis, delinquency, physical illness and, ultimately, madness.

Chapter 11

Dubious practices

There are certain aspects of working four dimensionally I should like to consider, although they may be regarded as questionable deviations from orthodox technique. The first is the use of silence. A number of writers have suggested that psychoanalysis has overlooked its value. Andrea Sabbadini wrote an expressive essay on the many kinds of silence that can flower within the session (Sabbadini 1991). Michael Del Monte (1995) compared it to the therapeutic use of meditation, in that it allows the analyst ample time to explore his countertransference. While language is among the greatest of human accomplishments, when it comes to the deepest issues of our lives speech finally fails; it even 'defiles', as the Zen teacher Daie remarked:

> To talk about mind or nature is defiling, to talk about the unfathomable or the mysterious is defiling; to practise meditation or tranquillization is defiling; to direct one's attention to it, to think about it is defiling; to be writing about it thus on paper with a brush is especially defiling.
>
> (quoted in Suzuki 1962: 165)

Traditionally the analyst has treated the silent patient as hostile, controlling, fearful or withdrawn, which he or she may well be, but not invariably. Balint wrote: 'if we can change our own approach – from considering silence as a symptom of resistance to studying it as a possible form of information – then we may learn something about this area of the mind' (Balint 1958: 328–40).

Equally often the patient experiences the silent analyst as massively intimidating. In everyday life a break in the continuity of conversation is often felt as threatening, a kind of social breakdown. The majority of people experience silence as intolerable and rush to fill it with noise of any kind, be it talk or music. One important experience derived from therapy, either individual or in a group, is learning to bear silence, and even to bask in it. In much of my case material I have suggested that phases of anxiety-free silence, where each party simply rejoices in the existence of the other, constitute a significant therapeutic experience. This may be a re-living of those early phases of quiet contentment in which the infant actually develops most rapidly (Stern 1985).

Between adults it requires an atmosphere of mutual trust which can evolve in the course of therapy. I notice that this can sometimes be facilitated by longer sessions. Winnicott allowed this with certain patients, for whom the mandatory fifty-minute hour was insufficient. In my own practice some patients who can only come once a week stay for ninety minutes, and up to two hours. This allows time for the venting and exploration of problems, after which the kind of silence described above may take over. The frequency of its occurrence seems to increase with time and with one or two patients it happens in every session. Although this altered state rarely occurs in normal interaction, it would appear to be simply the expression of a natural function. It has been commonly observed that people vary in their alertness at different times of the day: some are wide awake in early morning, others cannot rouse themselves without great effort. This is known as the circadian cycle which extends over a period of twenty-four hours. Recent research has discovered that about every ninety minutes to two hours throughout the day there also occurs a natural lowering of consciousness. This much shorter cycle is called the ultradian.

The significance of the ultradian cycle was noted by the Jungian analyst Ernest Rossi who had worked for many years in close co-operation with the eminent hypnotist Milton Erickson. He noticed that Erickson did not impose the familiar hypnotic techniques on his patients but utilised their own mental mechanisms. Erickson had a natural skill in noting the tell-tale signs when the natural ultradian rhythm was taking effect; he called these periods of quiet receptivity 'common everyday trance' which he could subtly enhance; he was then able to apply actively his therapeutic techniques (Rossi 1986).

My own response to these states, which are likely to occur within a two-hour session, is simply to share them and see what emerges. I am not sure if there is a process of mutual induction, or whether the patient's ultradian phase and my own sometimes simply coincide, but it seems to evoke a state in which, in Freud's words, 'unconscious may speak directly to unconscious' (Freud 1915). I find I may experience fantasies, or even somatic sensations, which belong primarily to the patient's inner life, or to an area that we both share. Or there may develop that particular concentration described by Bion as 'bringing to bear a beam of intense darkness upon the patient's associations'. There are times when both speech and silence become expressions of a 'third state' – one highly conducive to the patient's free associations, or to my uttering casually what Meltzer has called an 'inspired interpretation' (1979). On various occasions I find I have used a metaphor that, by sheer coincidence, exactly described an incident in the patient's past; or my patient might voice a thought on precisely the theme I had woken up thinking about that morning. It was as if, in this unstructured play-space, we each had access to the other's thoughts (Field 1989: 512–22).

The capacity to tune directly into another person's thoughts and feelings is not a rare gift but, given the appropriate setting and mental disposition, potentially available to everyone. For a number of years the researcher Henry Reed, who holds a professorship in Transpersonal Studies at Atlantic University, Virginia, has conducted workshops of between 50 to 300 people at a time, most of them strangers, testing the capacity for psychic contact. In all he has worked with about 4,000 people. The participants are asked to pair up and open their imagination to their partner. Reed takes them through an induction procedure of relaxation, tuning in, and letting go. Mutual attunement is facilitated by their engaging in brief face-to-face mirroring exercises. Thereafter they take it in turns, for a period of three minutes, to open their minds and hearts in silence to the other person. The overwhelming majority of participants testify that they have a subjective awareness of a distinct vibe, connection, atmosphere, energy, flow of warmth or cold from their partner or in the space between them. Some have fantasies, thoughts or physical sensations (such as a sudden toothache) which specifically relate to the partner's private experience.

> We both felt a bubble of energy between us.... There was a pulsation between us and then I felt we were surrounded by cold flames. My partner said she also experienced these things.... I saw her eye coming very close to mine until as

it swivelled I found myself looking into my face as if through her eyes.

In the course of the workshop, participants change partners, and learn that their rapport is greater with some than others, depending on each party's inner resistance.

> I felt vibrations that were unlike mine. The person was very afraid of coming close. The second person and I were very close, and had incredible energy between us that was shared – very intimate experience.
>
> (Reed 1996: 96–7)

Analogous communications spontaneously occur in the therapy setting. An admirable description is given by analyst T.H. Ogden in tracing his random, widely ranging and apparently meaningless associations while sitting in sterile silence with a patient. By skilful self-examination he was able to discover how his private ruminations actually reflected the inner thoughts of his patient; when he eventually shared them, his patient felt understood and received, and this took their work onto a much more productive level (Ogden 1994: 3–19).

Ogden conducted his private ruminations while awake. It frequently happens that, much to the therapist's embarrassment, he or she may feel overwhelmingly sleepy in the session:

> In one case where I was working with a scientist I dozed off during a long silence and had a dream. In it I was travelling on a bus to Hull, and then, once arrived at my destination, I found the bus taking me from Hull towards the south-west. I woke immediately after the dream and decided to tell my patient what I had dreamt. I asked him whether this dream meant anything to him. He said, 'Yes' immediately and told me that when he had left school he had very clear and fixed ideas about becoming a research scientist, and applied to Hull University for a place. He did not like the interview, nor the interviewer . . . although he was offered a place he altered his plans and decided to go to Exeter University in the south-west. . . . The connection of all this with his therapy lay in the fact that he did not know where his therapy was taking him next.
>
> (Harris 1993: 15)

ERROR AND RECOVERY

Another aspect of working in a four-dimensional spirit is conveyed by Winnicott's notion of 'failing the patient'. As in all creative activity, accidents sometimes happen. In painting, for example, the brush might drip; the artist does not necessarily erase the error but builds on it. Likewise in therapy errors of all kinds can occur: the therapist is late, or mistakes the hour of the session; the bill is incorrect; or the therapist attributes to the patient a remark he or she didn't make, a dream he or she didn't have, an event that happened to someone else. At the time the error can take on the proportions of a catastrophe; but it may be a blessing in disguise, an act contrived by the unconscious to move the work forward, not least by forcing the analyst to scrutinise the countertransference. A great many scientific breakthroughs, like the discovery of penicillin, have come about by accident. If we, as therapists, always throw away the mould and present only the jam, all kinds of discoveries may be lost or delayed. The following clinical episode illustrates how it proved possible to redeem a serious blunder.

Jane had been coming to see me for over four years and we had long before reached a sterile plateau where she seemed hopelessly stuck. Whatever brief alleviation of spirit might occur while she was with me was never sustained in the world outside. However disappointing, it did not occur to me to give up the treatment, but instead to redouble my efforts. Although sparing in her expressions of gratitude, Jane had more than once conceded that I was her 'lifeline' and, given the unremitting bleakness of her existence, this was hardly an exaggeration. Her relationship with me was virtually the only one she had. She came from another country, her parents were dead, and she had no contact with the remaining members of her family. She was unique in my experience as the only person I had met who did not have, and had never had, even one friend. She had reached middle age without making a single enduring relationship. She longed for a partnership with a man, but her fear of not coming up to expectation, her hair-trigger touchiness, her uncompromisingly critical faculties, plus an unyielding refusal to make any concession in either dress or manner, made such prospects seem extremely remote.

Friendships with her own sex were equally abortive: she resented older women who had authority over her and envied the younger ones who she saw as more attractive than herself. Indeed she was fearful of intimacy of any kind. Her working life was characterised by a thousand unforgotten acts of deprivation and neglect: when mid-morning tea was made in the office Jane often just got forgotten. Therefore it was all the more shocking that one day, when she arrived for her therapy, I was out. I had just forgotten.

It was mid-summer, and I had taken advantage of a cancellation to enjoy half-an-hour's stroll in the sunshine. Except that I stayed out for one and a half hours. Long after Jane had given up ringing my bell and gone, I suddenly remembered our usual appointment! My horror was acute. I telephoned her, again and again, my tormenting fantasies mounting with each unanswered call, until late in the evening I got through and expressed my apologies. I offered her a session the next day, which she declined; but, to my relief, she agreed to keep her next appointment.

In the days that followed, my mortification increased. How could I have perpetrated such a rejection on any patient, least of all Jane? Others regarded her as an irrelevant person but how could I, whom she regarded as her lifeline, treat her with the same contempt? When I confessed my blunder to a colleague, he too was aghast. My guilt developed into punishing ruminations about my competence to do my job: I wondered if my memory was failing. Or perhaps there was a core of sadism in me that analysis had never reached – or was even ineradicable. In short, should I give up forthwith? My guilt was like a fever; I tried to struggle through it, to make sense of what had happened. Why had I forgotten *Jane* of all people? There came the dimmest glimpse that, perhaps, *that* was the point – precisely because it *was* Jane. I began to face the painful possibility that, in spite of my conscious commitment to value her as a person, unconsciously I entertained the same indifference to her as everyone else. I too regarded her as an irrelevance. How could I admit to such a debased attitude, and worse, what would such an admission do to Jane herself? Even as I conjured up some plausible excuse for my lapse, I knew I had to tell her the truth.

It took several very painful sessions, and things were never the same again. Jane was profoundly hurt by my admission but, to my surprise, not actually destroyed. Apparently it was something she had half-suspected all along. What really got destroyed was her idealised image of me. But this enabled us to look at the split between us that had existed almost from the beginning: at one pole was this poor, wretched patient, drowning in envy, loneliness, despair, and frustration; at the other this supportive, empathic, lifeline of a therapist.

It may be asked if it was necessary for me to act out in such a gross way in order to expose this unsatisfactory situation. Surely our collusion could have been recognised and interpreted? In fact I had many times pointed out that the more she invested in me the more depleted she became. But this did not diminish her idealising transference; on the contrary it reinforced it. On top of all my other virtues, I was modest with it! I had further interpreted that she and I had recreated between us the split that had existed between her parents: her father so generous and popular, her mother so puritanical and self-hating, so deeply envious of her husband's warmth and self-confidence. As a couple they had been irreparably divided and this split had been recreated within Jane. Like a country ravaged by civil war, her inner world was dominated by her parents' conflicted relationship, like two armies laying waste the land. Whatever personal potential she might have developed had no chance to grow. In the transference I had been kitted out in her father's radiant mantle while she allotted to herself her mother's miserable sackcloth. When I put this to Jane she merely replied: 'That's all very interesting, but it doesn't change a thing.'

At different times we had explored how, as a little girl, Jane had longed to respond to the love her father bore her, but she dared not show it for fear of her mother's displeasure. In fact it went even deeper, since she could not cope with the love she sometimes saw in her father's eyes, as if she had no idea how to live up to it. Rather than risk alienating her mother, Jane made a tacit alliance against her father. Indeed she had little option, mother was always there while her father was at work or increasingly out and about; and when he died Jane became the companion of her mother's widowhood. It brought her a degree of security but no satisfaction, because she had nothing but contempt for her mother's bitter respectability, and refused to become the 'elegant' creature her mother wanted her to be. When I asked her to consider all this, Jane responded: 'That's history. It doesn't help me now.'

Jane's style of dress was so drab that the effect could only have been achieved by a resolute, lifelong determination to look unattractive. While she grudgingly accepted that her appearance was dictated by her determined opposition to her mother's image of how a woman should look, any reference to her clothes had in the past aroused such violent resentment that I never dared explore further. But now, in order to explain my blunder, I insisted on interpreting that, in spite of consciously rejecting her mother's petit bourgeois values, Jane had taken deeply into herself her mother's conviction that, as women, both she and her daughter were failures. It was this cruel introjection which I, in spite of my high-minded aspirations to the contrary, had taken in from Jane.

To this Jane said:

'Then you're no better than the rest.'
'I'm afraid that's true. It seems I was no better at withstanding your
       mother's judgement than you were.'
'Then you're no good to me.'

Since I had plainly rejected her, I could hardly blame Jane for rejecting me in turn. But here she was only half right, and somewhere she knew it. It was precisely because I was no longer so good that I could now, perhaps, be good *for her*. The forgotten appointment not only exposed the split between us, it diminished it by diminishing me; and not only in Jane's eyes, but in my own. It cracked my comfortable image of myself as the caring therapist, the human lifeline who kept Jane afloat. I had been trapped in that image, and Jane had been trapped with me.

It may have become evident that Jane's responses to my interpretations ensured they would have no beneficial effect. She simply nullified them; and the more apt they were, the more lethal her treatment. I now realised that behind Jane's idealisation lay an immense envy, and this led her to frustrate all my therapeutic endeavours, as if to say: 'You think you're going to make me better. Well, you've got enough going for you, without having me to be pleased about.' Indeed it was the unwritten agenda of her life: by failing at everything she had the perverse satisfaction of reminding her parents, even though they were dead, of how they had failed her.

With hindsight I began to realise that my forgetting her had been my retaliation. It brought a sterile therapy to the point where I thought it had totally broken down; but thanks to Jane's resilience, and my own readiness to be honest and persist in the work, it actually initiated a process whereby Jane began to free herself from her blemished identity.

Chapter 12

Danger in the fourth dimension

As may have become evident from much of the clinical material I have already presented, the blunder with Jane was not the only time in my practice when the therapeutic relationship looked near to collapse. It has been my experience on various critical occasions – when I have become utterly confused, have run out of interpretations, and feel at the end of my tether – to have to admit to my patient that, at this moment, I feel as helpless as they do. Although profoundly shaken, I have learnt to convey this neither as a reproach to the patient ('You have made me feel . . . '), nor to myself ('I'm dreadfully sorry but . . . '), but simply as a statement of how things are. Instead of going into even greater panic, most patients respond positively: 'Thank God someone understands what it's like to feel as hopeless as I do.' Or simply: 'If you can't see a way out, it doesn't feel so bad that I can't.'

Where the patient's distress is more profound there may be no such response and the period that follows is spent in depressed silence. It is as if neither of us can think of a thing worth saying. Yet our mutual helplessness is itself a powerful bond. If both of us are rendered dumb, at least we are dumb together. Hopeless silence is all we have and it feels vital to sustain it: in Bion's terms it is a shared negative realisation. If I feel this inner connection beginning to weaken I may enquire what is passing in the patient's mind in order to re-affirm the link between us. In these phases, if I speak, it is only to support the silence. Although I suffer moments of acute unease that I seem to be doing nothing, just sitting while the hour is passing, the fact is I have nothing useful to say. Intermittently I may find myself becoming drowsy; if both of us actually doze I begin to feel that something may soon develop. Presently the patient will report thoughts or fantasies of a different temper – that the room feels warmer, or the sun has come out – which often actually happens. There follows a marked sense of relief, sometimes expressed through the patient's tears, as if things are flowing again. Whereas empathic remarks were previously heard as criticism and carefully phrased interpretations got hopelessly misconstrued, there now exists a communicational matrix in which a therapeutic dialogue can take place. We are back in the third dimension.

From this point a positive rapport may now develop, a shared wellbeing, and it no longer matters whether we talk or are silent. There is a sense of communion, as with two people who have together lived through a crisis. Because the patient feels he or she has glimpsed the therapist's real self there is a deepening of trust. A male patient reported that he felt himself sinking into the couch and the couch was my body, as if he were returning to the womb. One woman patient enjoyed vivid fantasies of being back at the breast, lazily nuzzling and sucking as she felt inclined. Others have imagined that we were brother and sister, or perhaps twins in an earlier incarnation.

When I am sitting directly facing certain patients, and preferably with our eyes closed, an 'energy field' may start up between us. I have the distinct physical sensation that a flow of energy is emanating from my body towards the patient; the patient reciprocally feels theirs is flowing out and around me, even behind my chair, and links with mine. Sometimes the energy can be experienced 'like a solid ball' between us. It is as if our personal auras are joined and flowing in harmony. Schwartz-Salant is probably describing the same experience by saying the space becomes 'textured' (1986: 41).

This is a mysterious condition which feels healing and nourishing to both parties. Deeply agreeable though it is, it cannot be willed, and vanishes if there is an effort to control it, which is a great temptation. It is certainly unlike anything in normal experience, and could be envisaged as the quintessence of prolonged sexual union. A similar comparison to sexual bliss was made by the Indian mystic, Gopi Krishna, in describing his experience of the early phases of kundalini (Krishna 1970). Schwartz-Salant likewise notes the erotic charge, together with the sense of awakening:

> For one then moves out of a sphere of omnipotence in which the
> analyst knows more than the patient, and into a domain in
> which both people can discover how they have, so to speak,
> been acting out a mutual dream, or how they have been being
> dreamed.
>
> (Schwartz-Salant 1988: 50)

The mutual dream is the 'dream' of everyday life which only
becomes recognised with the awakening to another order of
reality. But access to it seems to be gained, more often than not,
via regressed states. This confronts us with the uncomfortable fact
that the higher and lower dimensions are paradoxically connected. When the patient's paralysed despair takes possession of
my mind I need first to re-find my capacity for thought, just to be
able to think: 'Right now *I can't think!*' Even this minimal grasp of
what is happening enables me to climb from the second into the
third dimension where sanity is restored. But to climb from the
third to the fourth the process needs to be reversed: I need to
inhibit my thinking processes and let a larger vision take over. But
this involves my being taken over by feelings of intense mutuality
– which may present another problem. If two people are spiritually united, why not physically also? After all, in everyday life
the combination of the sexual and spiritual is the basis of true
marriage, the pinnacle of human intimacy. But therapy is not
everyday life and it is a serious error to confuse the two. The
sacred can readily degenerate into the profane; that which could
heal may all too easily damage, and an opportunity for transformation is lost.

Many analysts, from Freud onwards, have warned against the
dangers of eroticised transference and countertransference, and
some of the most eminent practitioners have been susceptible to its
power, Breuer, Ferenczi and Jung among them. During Jung's time
as a psychiatrist at the Burghölzli Clinic in Switzerland a very
disturbed young woman came under his care: Sabina Spielrein.
From the evidence available it would appear that the treatment
generated an intense rapport between them, to the point where
each felt they could read the other's thoughts, or spontaneously
arrived at identical creative ideas. It is as if both fell under a spell;
Spielrein later wrote to Freud that she and Jung 'could sit in
speechless ecstasy for hours' (Carotenuto 1984: 96). A reductive
explanation would treat such states as a psychotic delusion, or the

incestuous aspect of an unconscious brother–sister pairing. In an earlier, more puritanical culture the 'imaginal' brother–sister couple might have been regarded as incubus and succubus, whom the Inquisition treated as emissaries of the devil. A medieval treatise on witchcraft intriguingly describes them as 'rampant and lickerish', having the same passions as men and women but with 'more tenuous and subtle bodies' (Williams 1963: 136).

This reference to subtle bodies seems to me significant. Just as a solid three-dimensional body casts a two-dimensional shadow, the 'shadow' of four-dimensional experience manifests as our familiar three-dimensional physical body: that is, the acting-out in physical terms of what is essentially a subtle body experience. In these phases of mutual bewitchment there can readily occur a confusion of dimensions, a category error. In the chakra system the sexual and the spiritual are essentially centres of energy, albeit at different levels of refinement. The ancient Eastern discipline of tantra, like alchemy, expressly uses sexual energy as a medium of spiritual transformation. But adepts are fully aware how such esoteric practices can degenerate into common abuse – those who exploit the situation for degraded purposes are actually described as 'brothers of the shadow'. According to Spielrein's letters to Freud her relationship with Jung did not remain on a purely spiritual level; she wrote that the 'inescapable' happened; at which point her lover became anxious and depressed. This was hardly surprising. Jung was not only a doctor who had now transgressed his Hippocratic oath, he was a married man and something of a celebrity. Under pressure from Sabina's mother he acted badly, disavowing his complicity in the relationship. Spielrein felt outraged at this betrayal of a love he had many times declared to her. She did not complain that she and Jung had sexually consummated their love, but at Jung's discreditable termination of it. While Jung had a professional responsibility not to take advantage of the passions he had aroused in his young patient, in her view the core of the abuse lay in his disavowal of what they had meant to each other.

Their story is instructive, in so far as there is increasing evidence of similar transgressions not only in the helping professions, but further afield (Rutter 1990). Sexual relations between male executives and female secretaries are a commonplace of business life. It also happens frequently between male divorce lawyers and their female clients; between male university instructors and female students; between ministers of religion and their flock. Very often it amounts to an abuse of power over a vulnerable woman by a man in authority, and recreates the daughter–father pairing. The relationship between therapist and patient is comparable to that between parent and child, and the betrayal of professional trust carries the stigma of incest. There is something archetypally offensive in a protector becoming an abuser: the topic is so highly charged that it can be difficult even to discuss it objectively without appearing to condone the abuse itself. Rutter certainly endeavours to show understanding: he readily admits to the strength of the temptation, and notes that there is a conspiracy of silence that surrounds the subject which, he suggests, indicates a widespread repressed inclination towards misconduct. At the root of it is the male fantasy that, through sex, through a return to the womb, through a renewed fusion with the mother, their childhood wounds will find healing. For the women who participate, intimacy with a man of power or spirit or intellect seems to offer a new life with boundless possibilities. Thus, for the male it is a going back, for the female a going forward. One of the many women Rutter interviewed expressed it thus: 'There is no doubt that what I felt was an almost indescribable combination of erotic-spiritual intensity. I felt as if Dr. M. almost physically had touched my heart. It was an ecstatic experience' (Rutter 1990: 24).

Each party seeks through the other to gain access to their own unrealised potential; both are possessed by a longing to get and to give; to heal and be healed. Rutter observes that:

> any relationship that moves us deeply, even if it is clearly nonsexual, can stimulate sexual fantasy. . . . What matters in the forbidden zone is not keeping sexual thoughts away, but maintaining a boundary against sexual contact so that the unique potential of these relationships can be realised.

This is a relatively liberal attitude; at one time there was a uniform reaction that any erotic response to a patient was not to be tolerated. Even now most analysts take a very guarded view of erotic transference–countertransference; but there are a few who have addressed the question more open-mindedly. Searles describes, in his characteristically transparent style, how, as his formerly unappealing schizophrenic patients began to get better, he began to feel tender, erotic and even romantic feelings towards them. He remarks:

I have come to believe there is a direct correlation between, on the one hand, the affective intensity with which the analyst experiences an awareness of such feelings – and of the unrealisability of such feelings – in himself towards the patient, and, on the other hand, the depth of maturation which the patient achieves in the analysis.

(Searles 1965: 291)

More recently David Mann has written perceptively on the subject, agreeing in the main with Searles's view that it is a vital part of the patient's development to excite desire in the therapist. But he disagrees that the therapist should acknowledge this desire to the patient (Mann 1994: 347). The Jungian analyst Robert Stein devoted a passionately argued book to the damage done by the withholding of a parent's loving feelings for the child which he called 'the incest wound', and likewise, the therapist for the patient. He is much more positive about personal disclosure and asks:

Will such mutual openness not tend to provoke concrete sexual involvement? In my experience this has not been the case. Quite the contrary. The less open and connected people are with each other, the more they feel compelled to act their sexual impulses in order to make a connection.

(Stein 1973: 162)

Another analyst, Andrew Samuels, is equally emphatic about the necessary role that a father's erotic feelings play in the enhancement of his daughter's personality:

If incest fantasy is acted out, it becomes destructive. But if it isn't there as an actual, concrete, tangible, bodily feeling in a real family, the literal family, then I do not think the kind of growth a girl can get out of her metaphoric relation with her father will take place (or a boy from his mother, for that matter). This is the implication of the idea that sexuality fuels the device that renders relationships into the stuff of inner growth.

(Samuels 1989: 80)

Because the relationship is invested with such value, it is all the more a betrayal when it degenerates into little more than an erotic diversion. Most of the women Rutter interviewed came to see themselves as damaged by the experience, and their former lovers as ruthlessly exploiting the power they had. This victim–abuser polarity seems to have transmitted itself to the author since, in spite of his understanding of the inner situation, he is inclined to treat all boundary breaking as male abuse, regardless of the quality of the particular relationship. In Jung's case it was the spiritual affinity which fuelled his sexuality, not the other way about. Those personally acquainted with Sabina Spielrein could observe no obviously seductive qualities in her; quite the contrary, she came across as formidably intense. So it was undoubtedly a very different quality that bewitched Jung. It is a cruel irony that something so intrinsically loving and creative should produce so much pain.

Their relationship lasted several years, during which time Spielrein became increasingly free of her symptoms, trained as a doctor and went on to become an analyst. It may have been Jung's readiness to meet her at the deepest levels of his inner life that was the crucial factor that mobilised her own healing potential. Nor did she, in spite of her disillusion, renounce her devotion to the qualities she had perceived in him.

In 1912 Spielrein came to publish a paper, 'Destruction as the cause of coming into being' (1994). In it she argues that 'Without destruction all coming into being is impossible' (1994: 174). In fact, she herself had the capacity to survive the destruction of the dreams she wove around her love for Jung and, by all accounts, she developed into a woman of exemplary character and out-standing gifts. Jung himself suffered the loss of Spielrein, which in turn contributed to the loss of Freud, as well as considerable loss of self-esteem, all of which helped plunge him into a long break-down. But he came out of it immeasurably deepened, and his most original work was distilled out of the whole experience.

In relating an episode where both parties emerged strength-ened from a potentially very damaging encounter, it is not my intention to condone the breaking of professional boundaries, any more than I approve of clinical blunders because they might lead to a breakthrough, or jumping off Golden Gate Bridge because it might produce a religious experience. Several women have come to me for treatment who had, in a previous therapy, been sexually involved with their therapists. Some had felt themselves cheated and abused, not so much by acts of sex as by the breakdown of the therapeutic situation. But not all felt they had been psychologi-cally damaged: that depended on the quality of the relationship.

This was totally contrary to my expectation. It led me to try to understand sexual acting-out in the same way as I had tried to understand other tabooed sexual activities, such as homosexuality, adultery and masturbation, all of which were at one time regarded with unthinking horror.

Robert Stein wrote:

> On principle, I do not recommend sexual involvement in the psychotherapeutic situation, yet I doubt that a young psychotherapist can learn to trust Eros and the sexual instinct if he or she is unable to risk this possibility. It is a danger well worth the risk. Better to be humanly vulnerable than perpetuate the dehumanising archetypal situation of classical analysis.
>
> (Stein 1973: 163–4)

In this I think Stein goes too far, but I would wish to affirm the possibility that even if the therapist has lost his heart he can still keep his head, so that even when all might seem irretrievably lost, if he can hold steadfastly to his therapeutic commitment, something can still be redeemed.

Chapter 13

Psychotherapy and subversion

The dangers attached to working in this personally committed way leads me to consider a greater danger concerning the whole therapeutic enterprise. Psychotherapy intervenes in the conflict that lies at the core of the human condition. I refer to the fact that our need for others and our need to be separate constitute two primary tendencies in human nature that cannot be readily reconciled. We are inescapably part of the human species; each of us was conceived in, born from, nurtured and reared by others, and only in the company of others can we grow to full human stature. But there exists an equally powerful need not to be solely a member of a family, community, nation, profession or group of any kind, but to be simply *oneself*. The failure of others to see, acknowledge, respect one's real self is felt to be the most destructive of deprivations. The search for the self is one of the rallying cries of modern society and a major reason for seeking psychotherapy. Hence it is hardly surprising that a successful analysis can result, for example, in a broken marriage.

Yet, in current therapeutic thinking, the benchmark of maturity is the capacity to make and sustain personal relationships. The development of object relations theory represents a significant advance on Freud's original drive theory, and there are few contemporary analysts who do not subscribe to it. Thus Bowlby concludes, at the end of his monumental study *Attachment and Loss*, that: 'Intimate attachments are the hub around which a person's life evolves' (1980). Fairbairn, a major theorist of object relations, stated that 'the greatest need of a child is to obtain conclusive assurance (a) that he is genuinely loved as a person by his parents and (b) that his parents genuinely accept his love' (Fairbairn 1952).

While this may be true for every child, it does not follow that
our exclusive need for object love remains unabated into maturity
and old age, by which time a certain capacity to be alone may be
regarded as an invaluable asset. For Fairbairn life begins and ends
in relationships: from 'immature dependency' to 'mature dependency' (Fairbairn 1952). Rarely, if ever, does he speak of self-
realisation; he seems to regard introversion is a form of schizoid
disorder, putting a pathological construction on a term which Jung
used in a purely descriptive sense. Jung himself, notwithstanding
his emphasis on the patient–therapist relationship, was far from
regarding human development as wholly encompassed within
the structure of personal relationships.

Ideally the capacity for relationships and the capacity for
individuation should complement one another, but is not always
the case. The most gifted and creative individuals are not
renowned for being the best parents or spouses; all too often their
vocation takes precedence over their domestic life. As Anthony
Storr's study *Solitude* (1988) so vividly depicts, many of mankind's
most original innovators, whatever their sphere of activity, had
great difficulty with long-term intimate relationships.

Another group of highly regarded individuals are the religious
mystics: the majority, being monks and nuns, never married. Some
of the greatest lived as anchorites, deliberately distancing themselves from society. St Paul avowed that it was better to marry than
to burn, and the Christian religious tradition has followed his
attitude in regarding human love as decidedly inferior to, if not the
enemy of, the love of God. The divergence between personal
relationships and personal vocation was rarely more sharply
illustrated than in the case of the Blessed Angela of Foligno who
expressly gave thanks for the death of her parents, her husband
and children because now she was 'free to follow God' (quoted in
James 1901).

The Jewish religious tradition is profoundly suspicious of
celibacy, and marriage is almost mandatory; but the real passion
of the great Hasidic rabbis was directed not to their wives (who
usually laboured in the kitchen or marketplace while their revered
husbands absorbed themselves in ecstatic prayer), but to God. It is
orthodox Hindu tradition for men of advanced age and spiritual
inclination, having fulfilled their worldly tasks, to become *sannya-
sin*; they renounce all family ties and possessions to dedicate their
remaining years to a life of poverty and prayer, aiming at enlight-

enment before death takes them. The weight of evidence does seem to suggest that deeply involving personal relationships are essentially incompatible with the higher reaches of individuation.

The obstacles to individuation bear more heavily on women than men. Society allots to each sex its expected role, but while men are free to follow a chosen career, women are trained to serve, nurture and relate – to partners, parents, children and friends. The lives of most women are embedded in the lives of others. Mrs B. was one of several women patients who, in middle life and with much guilt, came to therapy in order to discover *herself*; more precisely to discover that private, creative instrumental part of herself traditionally monopolised by men.

Given her aim, it is ironic that our therapeutic work was characterised by a transference so infantile and so prolonged that it seemed to defy explanation in familiar psychodynamic terms. The depth of her regression was all the more baffling in that Mrs B. was not, in any clinical sense, psychologically ill. She had a satisfying marriage and coped with a busy household of growing children while sustaining a demanding job in the social services. Nonetheless she had her problems: a tendency to take on too much and manage it in a controlling way that left her drained, and an enduring resentment against her mother. She came into therapy partly for personal reasons, partly as a continuation of her professional development. But these complications did not seem obviously connected with the emergence, as the transference deepened, of a needy, often desperate, helpless, enraged and apparently insatiable infant self that came increasingly to impinge on her tolerably well-functioning ego. Manifestly she came as a well, coping person and ironically got 'iller' as the therapy progressed.

Since no specific traumas had occurred in Mrs B.'s childhood, the greater part of our analytic work was devoted to searching out those early forms of deprivation, obvious or subtle, whereby her mother had failed her as a transformational object. Mrs B. was the first of two daughters, and there was considerable evidence that her mother was inexperienced and deeply insecure when she was born, and inclined to raise her rigidly by the book. Mrs B. recalled that she was brought up on a strictly mechanical feeding regime and put back into her cot with little or no time for talk, play or physical contact. Mrs B. was hardly more than two when her baby sister arrived.

Thereafter she was promoted to the role of little mother, which she accepted very readily; only much later did it emerge how much she longed for all the nursing her baby sister enjoyed. No matter how many times Mrs B. recalled her early months and years her rage and despair hardly abated; she could still hear the cry of that lonely infant left alone in its cot, longing to be picked up and cuddled. Her childhood envy of her younger sister, which led to Mrs B. secretly tormenting her, was extreme. Her unyielding negativity towards her now aged mother, irrational as she knew it to be, could still not be assuaged.

As a child Mrs B. managed to compensate by becoming daddy's best girl, although her father clearly tried to treat both daughters in an even-handed way. Father and daughter became close companions and she often accompanied him on daytime trips in the course of his job. It was a warm, wholesome relationship; he did sometimes reprove her, but usually in order not to break faith with his wife. Mrs B. adored him, but nevertheless managed to leave home to study, eventually found a good man of her own, and created a thriving family. When her father unexpectedly died in his late sixties Mrs B. was on holiday in a distant part of the country; her mother arranged the funeral very quickly and Mrs B. acquiesced in her advice that she need not attend and suffer undue distress. Years later she still bitterly regretted this, and felt she had not mourned his loss, which the therapy gave her an opportunity to do.

It was assumed by both of us that the inadequate mothering, further impoverished by the arrival of her baby sister, adequately accounted for the intense unsatisfied needs she felt within her. Yet I could not ignore the fact that her parents were essentially decent people, and her upbringing had been little different from the majority of children of her generation, mitigated, moreover, by a good relationship with her father. I could not quite escape the sense that this split in her – the deep rejection of her mother and her profoundly regressed attachment to me – remained not entirely explained by the deprivations of her infancy.

The most obvious manifestation of her dependency arose over my holidays: she agonised about them for weeks beforehand, felt abandoned in my absence, which resulted in blinding headaches. It took several intense sessions, after my return, for her to settle down. Her chief obsession about breaks was to know where I was going. I withheld telling her, not on principle, but from a feeling that her curiosity was intrusive. Over time it emerged her reason lay much deeper: the break in the continuity of our meetings was, as Winnicott described it in infants, virtually a break 'in the continuity of her being'. If only she knew where I was, she pleaded, she could imagine me in a place, hold me in her mind, and keep me alive. The reverse also held good: in the logic of primitive thinking, if she could hold me in her mind it meant that I held her in mine, and I thereby kept her alive. Both between and during sessions Mrs B. was possessed by a yearning for contact, for my voice, or my hand, or even a small gesture like tucking the blanket into her back, which again I repeatedly refused. Although I rarely touch a patient physically, I have no rigid rule that it must never happen. Yet in Mrs B.'s case I was aware of a marked reluctance to do so. I felt acutely uncomfortable about this with-holding, as if I was being wilfully sadistic. I strengthened my resolve by mulling over Patrick Casement's paper on the subject (Casement 1982) which stressed, in true psychoanalytic spirit, the therapeutic value of denying gratification. On further reflection I arrived at the notion that my reluctance to perform all these comforting services was introjected from Mrs B. herself: that she had projected into me a split-off withholding 'bad object' that she had introjected in childhood from her withholding mother. We came to an agreement that, if she could overcome this self-denying part in herself and actually ask for my hand, I would let her hold it.

Thereafter, while the analytic dialogue was unfolding in a seemingly adult manner, Mrs B. would be silently going through an agonising struggle: 'To ask? Or not to ask?' Frequently she never managed it, and on leaving would go into the toilet and cry. Sometimes she could ask easily, and I felt comfortable offering it. At other times, although she asked, I felt again that cold withholding, and said so. On exploration it emerged that instead of overcoming her internal 'bad' mother she had merely denied her and again split her off into me. I felt badly about refusing but I did; although disappointed, she felt I was right to do so, and even seemed relieved. While I consciously attributed my withholding feelings to projections coming from Mrs B., I was always vaguely uneasy that some triumphant sadism still lurked in me, unanalysed.

Much the same would apply to my verbal responses: there were many times when I felt acutely drowsy, incapable of thinking, almost stunned. I knew myself to be the recipient of massive projective identifications but could not, or would not, muster the energy to rouse myself. On these occasions she would lie on the couch, feeling utterly out of touch, and getting into near-hysterical states in her effort to connect with me. The harder she tried the more agonised she became. 'Help me,' she would plead, 'Say something.' When I replied that I really wanted to but just couldn't, she actually felt understood and calmed down. But sometimes I couldn't even say that much. In the continuing silence her desperation would mount: 'If only I could cry.' But she couldn't, any more than I could talk. It was tormenting for me but much worse for her, this struggle with something that seemed so little – just to 'be there' – yet which felt like a life or death issue. There was literally nothing either of us could do; we both knew she just had to stop trying and give up. But it was impossible for her to give up consciously. The process had to reach its own pitch of despair, and then it happened. Sometimes her tears would flow, or she would reach out for my hand, or simply say: 'Something has shifted ... I'm here.' I felt that when she connected with me she had reconnected with herself; as if she identified me with some essential part of her inner world. If there were still time remaining we would just stay silent: it felt amazingly peaceful and Mrs B. would have a calm, almost Buddha-like, expression on her face. The spiritual quality of the experience was reinforced by the conviction that this peace was not a manic escape, but a state of quietude that had always been there and was always waiting to be entered.

Sometimes this quiet was reached without any struggle; and I might then try to explore what fantasies were evoked in her mind. The most common was that we were a mother and baby: my hand was a breast and hers a mouth, and I drowsed while she fed. But equally important was her sense of being held: in her imagination each of my arms cradled her firmly from below so that she felt loved and utterly safe. This image invariably reminded me of a line from a hymn which ran 'underneath, the everlasting arms'. Her fantasy involved two simultaneous processes: holding and feeding.

Sometimes she manoeuvred my hand to lie on hers. This made me uncomfortable, as if our hands had become bodies and she was initiating a symbolic sexual encounter. When I voiced my unease she took fright and stopped. But I learnt it had quite a different meaning for her, not to be excited or penetrated but completed, to achieve a hermaphroditic fusion of the male and female elements. At other times she drew my hand to her cheek; this also seemed uncomfortably near to conventional adult tenderness. But again I made the wrong, adult deduction: it was not my hand stroking her cheek; it was her cheek nuzzling my breast, something she had never been allowed to do in infancy. I understood it, but never felt easy with it; again my failure of empathy, no doubt.

She had other persistent fantasies: of being picked screaming out of the cot, held close to my chest, and allowed to cry and cry. Whereas the feeding fantasies were of ingestion, these involved a massive evacuation of tears. They recurred in session after session, and would alternate with articulate explorations of adult matters, of family and professional problems, of various transference issues, such as her anger towards me, her envy of me, ways in which she might be manipulating me, and so on – all of which she could readily explore in the context of the holding situation. But if she felt unheld, no interpretation had any meaning.

By the fifth year of her analysis Mrs B. went back to sitting in the chair. It seemed to reflect a development to a more adult relationship. Patients often respond to helpful interpretations in a somatic way, such as a tummy rumble which suggests something is being digested. Mrs B. had her own way of reacting: she would uncross her legs and stretch out in her chair, so that her whole body seemed to smile, melt and open. Therefore it was not at all shocking when this devoted wife and mother arrived one day and, with almost no embarrassment, recounted her fantasy of a marvellous sexual encounter between us. It went in two phases: first we embraced face to face in the tenderest way imaginable and enjoyed a state of prolonged sexual fusion. Next I entered her from the rear and impregnated her with joyful and unabashed vigour.

I felt it a decisive development that, after years of seeing me as a nursing mother or protective father, she had the courage to recount this fantasy of passionate genital sexuality. With this disclosure I date the beginning of the end of the therapy, as if once she could relate to me as an adult she could leave. I made no attempt to repress within myself my enjoyment of her fantasy; on the contrary I felt able to share it, to affirm and honour it, and then try to transform it into understanding.

In her fantasy Mrs B. had described a twofold encounter: first she was held in the spirit of love and achieved a state approaching pure receptivity; then, in a spirit of pure lust, she was impregnated as naturally as an animal. On reflection, it seemed to me an adult version of her feeding fantasies; first she was held with a firmness that gave her total security, then was penetrated by the nipple and filled with life-giving stuff. Both fantasies re-enacted in bodily terms the two-fold process of creation: first the state of receptivity, then the impregnation. They equally reflected how she experienced the dual process of therapy: that of holding and interpretation. I have in mind interpretation as the active agent of transformation, as Freud originally conceived it. This would correspond to Bion's idea of the preconception mating with a positive realisation.

In Bion's theory there is an alternative scenario, where the infant's expectation meets a 'negative realisation', the absence of satisfaction. There could then ensue, providing the frustration can be tolerated, the paradigmatic leap to 'thought' – to the next level of development. I think this corresponds to those phases where Mrs B. felt utterly incapable of 'being there', when in fact neither of us were there, because she had rendered me incapable of thought. Although I had felt heartless at not rousing myself and coming to her rescue, with hindsight I could see it was vital that I did nothing, that I let the therapy break down, so that we reached the shared recognition there was nothing either of us could *do*. But by enduring this phase, by giving up yet hanging on, something shifted in the unconscious, a connection was made, whereupon life and meaning flowed back into the session. Winnicott described the same process in the patient's need to destroy the object in order to find that it survives.

While much of the power behind Mrs B.'s positive transference can be traced to her childhood love of her father, I take the view that her innate need to 'realise her animus' lent it a special tenacity and intensity. In the context of the therapy relationship Mrs B., while wholeheartedly committed to her husband and family, had a special kind of 'love affair' with me. More precisely it was a love affair of 'self with self' in that what she attributed to me was a projected aspect of herself, something she saw as male, active, clarifying, the embodiment of her innate masculine potential. There was never any doubt, either on her part or mine, that in her fantasy she and I were an *imaginal* couple: neither of us confused our carnal with our subtle bodies. I see the power of her fantasies as the measure of her deep spirituality; by which I mean, her passion for wholeness and individuation. Loving sex is the commonest means whereby we seek to transcend the self and become one with a particular individual who seems to embody what we most treasure – ultimately the unrealised aspect of ourselves. If, as Fairbairn says, pleasure is the signpost to the object (Fairbairn 1952: 33), in Mrs B.'s fantasy sexual love served as the signpost to her soul.

There were times when, in the transference, Mrs B. saw me as a mother, more often as a father, but at the deepest level as her *animus*. Freud's psychoanalytical model of the transference focuses on the parent–child dyad, whereas Jung's alchemical model assumes a male–female polarity. This difference of focus has significant implications. In the psychoanalytic model the child introjects the parental values in the form of the superego; this, it is hoped, makes for greater maturity, and thereby for better object relationships. In the Jungian alchemical model it is the anima (or animus, as the case may be) that is first projected, then re-introjected. In so far as this makes for the realisation of the receptive (feminine) aspect in a man and the dynamic (masculine) aspect in a woman, the process is one of becoming whole through the introjection of one's contrasexual potential. In broad terms, Freud's parent–child model of transference promotes object relationships, whereas Jung's brother–sister pairing model tends to facilitate individuation. In Mrs B.'s case, although a profound change had undoubtedly taken place, I find it difficult to evaluate the outcome of several years of intensive psychotherapy. Her negative attitude to her mother abated considerably but was never quite resolved. Although her positive transference to me had persisted year after year, she did come to see me more nearly for what I was in myself. Yet some deep bond remained between us, as if we were imprinted upon one another for life. The yearning fantasies of crying on my lap, which we analysed time and again, just wore themselves out and were forgotten, rather as an old teddy bear eventually loses its magic and lies forgotten at the back of a cupboard. At the same time I had the paradoxical impression that, as ever more regressive elements came into awareness, her personality matured, her professional status improved, and above all she came to enjoy her husband and children a great deal more. As the part she had projected into me was progressively re-introjected she could love her real-life partner for what he was in himself; he was no longer required to provide that missing part of herself. With increasing integration of her contrasexual potential, her deep uncertainty about herself became replaced by a quiet self-confidence: she had become a person of authority. So, while her capacity for relationship was enhanced, the growth in individuation had made her more separate. Much was gained, but perhaps something was also lost. It raises the question whether the drive to be oneself is a healthy impulse, or merely an extension of our narcissism. The tension between relating and individuating raises the whole question of what we actually understand by pathology.

Chapter 14

What is psychopathology?

The great variety of psychopathological symptoms were identified by psychiatry well over a century ago. They include chronic anxiety, irrational fears, obsessionality, neurotic guilt, shame and hysteria; phobic, panic, manic and depressive states; the whole spectrum of psychosomatic illnesses; behavioural disorders that manifest as perversion, violence and delinquency; disorders of perception such as delusions and hallucinations; as well as disorders of affect such as schizoid, borderline and schizophrenic states. Many of these conditions alternate or appear in combination and manifest in varying degrees of intensity. But varied as they are they fall into two main categories: they are either the expression of our most primitive instincts, such as rage, lust, and fear; or they are the expression of equally primitive defences against them. These psychoanalysis has identified as splitting, projection and projective identification. Each of us, in infancy, resorts to these defensive mechanisms in order to mitigate the intense psychic pain that inevitably comes with being an infant. According to Fairbairn we are all, at the deepest level, schizoid (1952: 3–27). Put more provocatively: none of us is normal.

It is a fact that all these infantile phenomena – both the primitive instincts and the primitive defences – can readily be observed in mental illness. But does it follow that infancy itself is a form of illness, which seems to be implied by Klein's characterisation of early mental states as the 'paranoid-schizoid position'? Since there are normal and sick infants, the matter must necessarily be more complicated.

In support of Klein there is a formidable body of opinion that regards the human mind as inherently flawed. It is implicit in the biblical story of the Fall which tells us that ever since Eve yielded to temptation in the Garden of Eden we, her offspring, have all been born with the blemish of Original Sin. Arthur Koestler offers a scientific version of the same attitude when he suggests that the human species is very likely one of evolution's non-viable experiments. Our innate defect arises from the disjunction between the cortex of the human brain with its marvellous intellectual capacities, and the original reptilian brain stem which underlies it. Given such a combination of primitive violence and intelligence he thinks it highly possible that the human species will destroy itself (Koestler 1967).

The analyst Otto Rank regarded human nature as flawed on the basis that none of us ever recovers from the trauma of birth; deep down none of us wishes to leave the safety of the womb and unconsciously longs to get back (Rank 1924). An alternative hypothesis derives from the work of Stanislas Grof, who did extensive research on the effect of high doses of LSD, which brings pre-natal memories into consciousness. The reactions of his subjects suggested that, in the actual process of birth, each of us inevitably suffers terrifying distress in squeezing through the narrow birth canal: this repressed memory acts like a lifelong trauma in the unconscious (Grof 1979). Fairbairn, by contrast, asserts that we are all born without blemish but the damage inevitably occurs afterwards (1952: 59–81). However empathic our parenting, since it cannot be perfect, none of us can quite escape becoming schizoid: that is, we defensively split off into the unconscious a part of our personality and lose our primary wholeness.

But when Fairbairn tells us that 'at the deepest level' we are all schizoid, he is evaluating mental health against some ideal standard; his hypothetically unblemished Central Ego. Fairbairn, like the ancient Taoist philosophers or the biblical story of Paradise, places the ideal state in the past. By contrast, Aristotle's concept of a Final Cause locates it in the future: namely that the 'real' nature of a thing is what it can become. One way or another, they all subscribe to an *ideal* meaning of normality.

But to assert that none of us is normal is to forget that some are more normal than others, so it would seem that we are using the word 'normal' in two different senses. Any meaningful evaluation of normality must take into account whether a thing is a good or bad example of its kind. This is the *comparative* criterion. An ape is not an inferior man; it is an ape. Yet apes themselves can become mentally disturbed: confine them for any length of time in an overcrowded environment and they show a marked increase in violence, homosexual coupling and a decrease in breeding.

When we dream at night we enter a world that, from the viewpoint of waking consciousness, may be utterly irrational. But that does not make dreaming a form of madness. Another of Freud's great discoveries was that dreams function according to their own laws, condensation, displacement, reversal, etc. Dreams, like apes and infants, can themselves be normal or pathological. Dreaming, as a primary human function, so far from being evidence of madness, appears to be vital to human health. The evidence for this emerged from laboratory dream research when it was observed that experimental subjects, repeatedly awakened as their dreams began, started to show increasing neurotic symptoms. When allowed to sleep undisturbed, their dream activity became deep and prolonged, as if urgently making up for lost dreamtime; after which they returned to their former normality.

But although the comparative evaluation of normality must be taken into account, it too is fraught with anomalies, since the notion of normality varies in every generation and with every culture. Behaviour that was outrageous a hundred years ago is broadly acceptable now, and vice versa; what is normal today in Amsterdam is criminal in Amman. It is a sociological commonplace that we readily label as mad or bad any sort of conduct or thought that deviates from our particular cultural norm. When the deviancy is directed at others it is called a crime; when it is directed at oneself it is termed mental illness.

The comparative evaluation of normality becomes especially problematic when an entire family can be shown to function pathologically while the member presented as sick proves to be the one closest to reality (Laing and Esterson 1964). It is equally valid to judge an entire sub-group, such as the Mafia or Gestapo, as mad or bad when compared with civilised norms. Yet each of these 'societies' has its own very strict code of morality, especially with regard to loyalty to the group. Under the Soviet regime political deviants were subjected to drug treatment which, simply by reducing the individual's level of mental functioning, converted them into good Soviet citizens. Who then was insane, the certified patients or the psychiatrists who dutifully administered the drugs? In the face of these complexities it has been argued that there is really no such thing as psychopathology; that the term is simply a device whereby the establishment, whether communist, capitalist, religious or psychiatric, stigmatises, disenfranchises and imprisons its deviant members.

Yet this cannot be the whole truth. Simply to be in the company of an autistic or hyperactive child, a paranoid schizophrenic or clinically depressed adult, is to be in the unmistakable presence of mental illness and the misery it involves. Let us compare two hypothetically distinct personality types: a contented labourer with a tormented artist. We will assume that our amiable labourer aspires to nothing, has achieved nothing, gives no one any trouble, and lives quietly with his mother. While she is alive, he will never present for treatment because he has no problems. He is not normal only in the sense that he has failed to develop to adult stature.

By contrast the artist drinks and smokes to excess and hates himself for it. He is physically very fearful but compulsively attracted to violence. He repeatedly falls in love and is repeatedly hurt. If anyone does come to care about him he becomes unaccountably bored and hostile, and rejects them. He only wants what he doesn't have, and what he has he doesn't want. Most of the time he is either manic or depressed, victim or bully, brooding over the past or fantasising about the future. Apart from those infrequent creative phases when he is actually painting, his entire being is torn apart by opposing impulses. Is it not justifiable to diagnose him as a neurotic, a hysteric, perhaps even schizoid, and leave it at that?

From a comparative viewpoint this is valid; his relationships with others, and with himself, are riven with conflict. But from the ideal or developmental perspective it is not quite so simple: difficult he may be, but he is always stimulating. And must we assume that conflict is equivalent to illness?

In fact, everything that we know we can only know by means of opposites: we conceive of space in terms of up and down, long or short, inside or outside. Our sense of time is constituted by past and future; of moral life in the distinction between good and bad; of society in the polarity between self and others; of our personal existence in terms of life and death. Splitting, in this sense, is an essential human characteristic that makes knowledge possible. But splitting has had a bad name from time immemorial: man's original sin, which the Bible calls 'the knowledge of good and evil', was simply the acquisition of consciousness, and this involves the splitting of the knower from that which is known, the sundering of humankind from God.

Each of the major depth psychologists has presented his or her discoveries in terms of complementary opposites. Some are expressed in concrete terms: mother/baby, parent/child, penis/vagina, nipple/mouth. Others are more abstract: conscious/unconscious, male/female, mind/body, extraversion/introversion, envy/gratitude, container/contained, and so on. Freud's dual drive theory recognised two primary instincts: the sexual and the aggressive (1912). They are themselves complementary: the former seeks to preserve the species, the latter the individual. Drive theory is itself complemented by object relations theory: the first concerns the subject, the second the object; one deals with causes, the other with goals.

Splitting, while it may turn pathological, must be regarded as a process essential to becoming human. The same applies to the other primitive defence mechanisms, such as projection, projective identification, and the introjection of primary objects. It applies equally to our primitive instincts: aggression, sexuality, narcissism, dependency. They are our natural endowment. As infants they are almost the whole of us, and that is health, but as we mature they must become part of us, the servant of our evolving ego, or they become pathology. Pathology occurs when the servant controls the master, the lower the higher, the part the whole.

In practice many original discoveries about human nature have been made by psychoanalysts in the course of their clinical work. This meant that they were observed first in their pathological aspect, and only with further exploration were they seen to be distorted expressions of natural functions. Freud regarded *transference* first as an obstacle, then as central to the therapeutic method; the *countertransference* too he saw as an 'obstruction to the analyst's understanding' and it was left to others, originally Paula Heimann, to see its creative possibilities (Heimann 1960). Klein first identified *projective identification* as a pathological defence mechanism (Klein 1946); later she and her co-workers, notably Bion, differentiated the normal from the pathological aspect of projective identification and elevated it to the status of a basic developmental process. Just as projective identification is now recognised as the foundation of all human empathy, so another much maligned primitive function, *concrete thinking*, seems due for reappraisal as a necessary ingredient in art, imagination and metaphor. *Narcissism* is still regarded as a basic personality disorder, yet in recent years Rosenfeld (1964: 169–79) could speak of 'negative narcissism' and Kohut (1965: 243–72) based his whole system on the notion of 'healthy narcissism'. I remarked earlier that Fairbairn explicitly treated *introversion* as equivalent to schizoid pathology, whereas for Jung it has long been a healthy counterbalance to extraversion.

In his illuminating *Dictionary of Kleinian Analysis*, Robert Hinshelwood uses the phrase 'The primitive (or psychotic) defence mechanisms' (Hinshelwood 1991: 122) which equates the primitive and the pathological. But it needs to be clearly understood that primitive defence mechanisms are not, in themselves, psychotic; they are simply primitive and, like dreams, operate according to different laws from adult waking consciousness. Edna O'Shaughnessy differentiates thus: 'Defences are a normal part of negotiating the paranoid-schizoid position....Defensive organisation is a pathological fixed formation' (O'Shaughnessy 1981: 359–69). Defensive organisation describes a situation where the protectors have set up a protection racket, a mafia as much to be feared as the gangsters they claim to keep at bay. In Fairbairn's terms the innocent Central Ego has become the victim of the bad internal objects who are at war with each other. In clinical depression the 'anti-libidinal' mafia has taken control; in manic states, the 'libidinal' gangsters have ousted them. Whichever side is in control its enemy is always waiting; and all the time the terrorised ego is trapped in the crossfire and systematically bled dry.

I think it is important to clarify that neither the primitive instincts nor the primitive defences are in themselves pathological; they are simply one-dimensional. Each of the dimensions I described earlier is a stage of normal development that can become pathological if the lower dominates the higher; for example, Melanie Klein's notion of the paranoid-schizoid position refers to the pathological aspect of the two-dimensional level when the primitive has taken over. Psychotherapy is most familiar with the pathology of the second and third dimensions, where the rational ego is overwhelmed by the primitive instincts or defensive organisations. But pathology can occur at any level, including the four-dimensional. Many otherwise spiritual persons become sick if they allow their special gifts to be subverted by inferior tendencies, as when adulation leads to inflation. It may be very difficult to differentiate between inspiration and nonsense, visions and delusions, between martyrdom and masochism, between the ecstasies of a 'bride of Christ' and orgasmic hallucinations.

These two quite distinct scales of assessment, the ideal and the comparative, reflect the distinction I drew in the preceding chapter between individuation and object relating. The ideal scale embraces such notions as introversion, self-actualisation, personal potential; it takes note of such difficult-to-measure qualities as aliveness, meaningfulness, complexity of organisation, richness of personality, creative skills, intellect and ultimately spiritual development. The comparative scale is concerned with extraversion, with the quality of relationships, with the capacity to live with others in a mutually fulfilling way, with the degree of conflict between parts and the whole of the self.

I have argued that there is an inherent antagonism between the two, that the liberation of personal potential does not necessarily produce a reliable parent or loving partner. All too often it may result in breaking up a lifelong relationship. A man entered into therapy with me very recently, having been urged to do so by his wife. But the therapy itself rapidly became another source of conflict between them: the husband was prepared to come on the understanding it would be an open-ended process of self-exploration; the wife, deeply committed to the comparative position, insisted the aim must be to strengthen the marriage and restore him into a loving partner; anything else was blatantly 'selfish'. Yet from his 'ideal' viewpoint it could be argued that to be merely a good parent, partner or citizen is itself a limited aspiration.

Joseph Campbell observed:

Psychoanalysis is a technique to cure excessively suffering individuals of the unconsciously misdirected desires and hostilities that weave around them their private webs of unreal terrors and ambivalent attractions; the patient released from these finds himself able to participate with comparative satisfaction in the more realistic fears, hostilities, erotic and religious practices, business enterprises, wars, pastimes and household tasks offered to him by his particular culture. But for the one who has deliberately undertaken the difficult and dangerous journey beyond the village compound, these interests, too, are to be regarded as based on error. Therefore the aim of religious teaching is not to cure the individual back again to the general delusion, but to detach him from delusion altogether.

(Campbell 1988: 164–5)

As psychotherapists we aim to heal psychic wounds, integrate splits, make the unconscious conscious, release unrealised potential, facilitate maturity, and so on, but we need to recognise that the path of self-realisation does not lead to a blissful, conflict-free plateau of existence. Progress to a new level inevitably leads us into new problems. Schopenhauer gloomily observed that human nature is so constituted that no sooner is one desire satisfied than another arises to take its place. The steep path of development, whether material or spiritual, is littered with the casualties of failed transformations.

Must depth psychology face the likelihood that it has no agreed notion of normality but confuses, and simultaneously pursues, two mutually contradictory goals? This may well account for its failure to live up to its original expectations. In trying to reach a basis for the evaluation of health and pathology, we must first face the fact that human development is a complex issue. It seems to involve the paradoxical pattern that we have to go back in order to go forward, and when we go forward we are in constant danger of going back. Is it possible to reconcile the ideal and the comparative scales – or any of the other polarities discussed in this book – and arrive at a conceptualisation that takes account of both?

The first step is to recognise that each scale is a linear concept. If we aim to integrate them, to give some sort of shape to paradox, we need to think in another dimension. We need to shift from the familiar model of, say, a two-dimensional graph which fits so comfortably on the printed page, to the more complex notion of something like a spiral. It is interesting to note that the spiral is a significant configuration. Historically it appears as the caduceus, a winged wand entwined by two serpents, the wand of Hermes which is the ancient symbol of healing. The spiral also appears as the double helix which depicts the molecular structure of the DNA molecule, as well as the spiral shape of the galaxies. In tantric mysticism 'kundalini', the coiled snake, represents the slumbering power of nature which, in the developmental process, unwinds in an ascending spiral up through the subtle body. Jung, too, recognised a spiral progression in the individuation process:

> The way is not straight but appears to go round in circles. More
> accurate knowledge has proved it to go round in spirals ... we
> can hardly help feeling that the unconscious process moves
> spiral wise round a centre, gradually getting closer, while the
> characteristics of the centre grow more and more distinct.
>
> (Jung 1944: para. 35)

Jung's image presupposes a flat spiral that progresses by slowly
moving around and towards a centre. Zinkin noted that there are a
multitude of configurations the spiral can take: long or short,
narrow or broad, cone or vortex, balanced or distorted (Zinkin
1979: 45). My own more workaday image of human development
is of a spiral path winding around a mountain shrouded in cloud.
Our contented bachelor, together with his fellows, sits snugly
holed up in a cave somewhere near the base, while the tormented
artist struggles blindly along the fog-bound track. At odd moments, through a break in the cloud, he catches a breathtaking
glimpse of a radiant landscape, but for the most part he keeps
stumbling on through the same difficult terrain, never knowing
whether he is going up, down or simply round in circles. He
struggles on, in the hope that it gets clearer and smoother higher
up, but this may be a complete delusion. And should he ever reach
the top, where can he go from there?

Chapter 15

Psychotherapy reframed

It was my original intention to organise the various themes of this book into a logical picture, one leading naturally to the next. But in practice this has proved more difficult than I anticipated. It was as if the material itself resisted this kind of sequential ordering and each section tended to become an exploration of similar themes from a succession of different perspectives. Instead of the clear linear argument I had aimed at, the direction of my argument seems to have assumed a shape nearer to that of a spiral. Thus the structure echoes the content which, in one sense, is about the integration of linear and cyclic processes.

In regard to the theory and practice of psychotherapy, these processes have been explored in terms of a dialectic between interpreting and relating; fathering and mothering; exorcism and healing; relationship and individuation; and between comparative and ideal scales of normality. These polarities, in turn, reflect the tension between classical science and quantum science; between 'causal–reductive' and 'prospective–systemic' forms of explanation; between science and religion. The last turn of the spiral leads now to a question long familiar to psychotherapists, and implicit throughout this book: is analytic psychotherapy a form of treatment or a way of life?

It is a fact of history that the founder of psychoanalysis was a doctor and the majority of leading depth psychologists have all been medically trained, so it would seem self-evident that analysis is a form of treatment. From its very beginnings it has been dominated by the medical profession and remains so to the present day. Psychotherapy is regarded as a form of treatment and those who receive it are still called 'patients'. Freud explicitly compared the attitude of the analyst to that of the surgeon. While there may be sound reasons for this we need to recognise that it has imposed on psychoanalysis the basic assumptions of medicine: namely that it must meet the criteria of natural science and must aim at the relief of pain, the cure of illness, and the preservation of life. But, on closer inspection, these may be assumptions not wholly applicable to psychological disorder. The therapist can only undertake to treat, never to cure; some degree of psychic pain may be necessary in that treatment; and even the preservation of life itself may be debatable in certain circumstances.

Implicit in the medical relationship is the assumption that the doctor, through specialist knowledge of the workings of the body, knows best; likewise it has been assumed that because the analyst has a special knowledge of the workings of the mind, he or she must always know best. But it is generally conceded that this highly unequal relationship may not be best suited to the therapeutic process. Nor does it conform to clinical reality, since the patient plays a vital role in the outcome.

> Freud's background as a neurologist in the logical–positivist tradition ... [arrogated] to the field of medicine the standards, criteria and authority of judgment over its credibility and practice, rather than to psychology, or for that matter, philosophy.
>
> (Grotstein 1992: 182)

Like any scientist of his generation Freud assumed the exclusive operation of causality; and one of his major contributions to modern consciousness has been the widespread recognition of how much childhood conditions adult life. The detailed exploration of a patient's early years is central to every analytic treatment. This aetiological approach is characteristic of the medical model, and integral to classical science. From Freud onwards every major analyst could confer no greater praise on his or her calling than that it was scientific: that is, rational, based on objective observation, and capable of reliable prediction. Jung was no exception: repeatedly in his writings he emphasises that he speaks as a scientist and physician and no mere metaphysician. Yet some hidden metaphysic exists in every conception we entertain:

> the psychotherapist carries on his work with an almost wholly unexamined 'philosophical unconscious'. He tends to be

ignorant, by reason of his highly specialised training, not only of the contemporary philosophy of science, but also of the hidden metaphysical premises which underlie all the main forms of psychological theory. Unconscious metaphysics tend to be bad metaphysics. What, then, if the metaphysical presuppositions of psychoanalysis are invalid, or if its theory depends on discredited anthropological ideas of the nineteenth century?

(Alan Watts 1971: 14–15)

From the very inception of psychoanalysis serious attacks have been made against its claims to be a science. One is a critical study by Grunbaum; amongst many formidable arguments, he points out that clinical data derived from psychoanalysis is irretrievably contaminated by transference and cannot seriously claim to be objective (Grunbaum 1944). An equally challenging overview of both analytic theory and practice was adopted by Farrell. He carefully sifted a wide range of clinical and theoretical considerations and reached the following conclusion:

Of course, it is disappointing to find that the method is of doubtful and limited value as a tool of exploration and discovery. It is equally disappointing to find it is of limited worth as therapy. This is especially so after the great hopes that were entertained in the early years of analysis.

(Farrell 1981: 207)

Nonetheless Farrell seems hesitant to pronounce sentence of death and consign psychoanalysis to the common grave of 'archaic and historical curiosities'; instead he holds out the vague hope that some time in the future some of the theory may be incorporated into science. A massive amount of experimental research has been devoted to testing the scientific credibility of Freudian theory, some of which has stood up well. These include the importance of the earliest developmental stages, the oral and anal in particular; the manifestation of the Oedipus complex; evidence of castration anxiety in boys, and some connection between paranoia and male homosexuality (Fisher and Greenberg 1985). By contrast, Freud's seduction theory, the drive theory, theories on the sexuality of women, the notion that we dream in order to stay asleep, all these and others have fared poorly when tested in the field.

It has become increasingly evident that psychological illness cannot be understood only in terms of cause and effect. While it is undeniable that the past profoundly affects the present, this is not the whole story. What Adler and Jung introduced into psychotherapy, each in his own way, was the notion of purpose. Adler based his whole system on the purposive overcoming of inferiority and defect. Jung regarded the psyche as a self-regulating organism; confronted by a patient's symptoms, he did not only ask: 'What caused this?' or 'How can we get rid of it?' but 'What can it be *for*?' (Jung 1954: 10). There is now virtually a consensus among depth psychologists of every school than linear causation cannot furnish an adequate explanation of human behaviour, although how to formulate an alternative still eludes definition.

Freud originally entertained the highest hopes that his psychoanalytic method could solve the massive, age-old problem of the psychoneuroses. Through experience he came to recognise that its use was limited to those with a capacity for insight, and even they, thanks to the negative therapeutic reaction, were often resistant to improvement. Some of his most celebrated cases were in fact therapeutic failures: the famous Wolf Man, whom Freud felt he had cured with a second period of treatment, made it clear in his memoirs that he continued to suffer severe psychological disturbances for the rest of his life.

Farrell's point about its 'limited worth as therapy' is supported by experimental research into the outcome of psychoanalysis. The broad consensus of experimental studies rates its therapeutic benefit as no higher than other, less intensive, therapeutic methods (Smith, Glass and Miller 1980). Most practitioners of the psychoanalytic method would not dispute these facts but argue that its central focus is not really about curing mental illness. It deliberately differs from other forms of psychotherapy in its rigorously self-imposed restrictions; it avoids offering any kind of corrective emotional experience, it does not try to compensate for early emotional deprivation; it makes no direct attempt to support a patient's fragile ego or to mitigate a punitive superego; it seeks only to clarify unconscious conflicts. The explicit goal of psychoanalysis is the original Delphic command: Know Thyself. It aims at nothing less than understanding and truth; when healing occurs, and it undoubtedly does, it happens as a by-product.

To suggest that insight plays little part in the healing process would be as partisan a view as the claim that it is the sole therapeutic factor. A clear-cut correlation between therapeutic technique and outcome has proved notoriously hard to pin down, but the broad sweep of outcome research seems to indicate that psychological healing depends less on any specific method and more on the quality of the relationship between the therapist and client, a finding which few patients will greet with surprise.

My own view of the matter is more complex and less gloomy than Farrell's: once analysis can concede that its curative capacities are limited and that the relief of symptoms may occur as a fortunate by-product, we can then ask in what profound ways it actually does change those who engage in it. Once we can take psychoanalysis out of its exclusively medical–scientific framework we are free to ask to what other types of discourse it might naturally belong.

One contemporary school of thought, presented with admirable lucidity by Charles Rycroft (1985) in the UK and Gregory Bateson (1972) in the US, regards psychoanalysis as a form of communications theory. The French philosopher, Foucault (1981), mindful of the descriptive aspects of psychoanalysis and its preoccupation with life and meaning, locates it in the philosophical tradition of existentialism and phenomenology. Those who actually practise analysis are deeply aware that it is as much an art as a science: thus we might compare the analyst's room to a stage, in that it is a place set aside from everyday life, while the analytic session, like a play, occupies a fixed space of time within which past and future are constellated in the transferential present. The analytic hour conforms precisely to the unity of time, place and action that Aristotle prescribed for drama. Earlier in the book I compared it to two instrumentalists engaged in a free improvisation. Psychotherapy has affinities with each of these disciplines, but if we view it from a historical perspective, I would argue that its roots are most deeply intertwined with those of religion; and its future, if we look at the developments of the present century in both science and depth psychology, lies in the facilitation of human potential. I am arguing therefore that it is essentially a way of life, with treatment as a beneficial side effect.

Classical psychoanalysis is based on the assumptions of classical science which itself, in the context of quantum theory, applies to an immense but *finite* number of cases: not, that is, to the very large or the very small. By the same token, Freudian theory and practice, based on the Oedipus complex, works very well in many cases, but not all; not with the category of patients commonly termed borderline, narcissistic, schizoid, namely those who Winnicott would regard as not having achieved 'unit status'. To Freud this limitation would present no difficulty: from the beginning he made it plain that psychoanalysis could be of use only to those who had reached a certain level of development. Since he had no intention of deviating from his method, he was very cautious about the prospects for the others. But in so far as we all, without exception, have a schizoid core to our personality, it is unlikely that any therapeutic treatment will not, at some point, encounter this level of primitive functioning. The surgical probe of insight cannot melt this frozen core; it can be reached only by the therapist's own heart and soul, which is what Jung meant by 'coniunctio' and Bion by 'at-one-ment'. None of this is news to either patients or the majority of psychotherapists and psychoanalysts currently in practice. The post-Jungian analyst James Hillman explicitly regards psychotherapy as a search for the soul (1972). His is not a lone voice but could be echoed by psychotherapists of every persuasion. The post-Winnicottian writer Adam Phillips envisages a state 'beyond the depressive position'; he contemplates going beyond object relations to a different dimension of being. 'It is one thing,' he says, 'to recognise the object – another person – as separate and to make him available for use, and quite another to live in time and make accidents available for use' (Phillips 1993). The Buddhist teacher Trung-pa phrased it very succinctly when he said: 'Situations are my guru.'

Expressions of this attitude, echoed by contemporary analysts such as Eigen, Arden, Levenson, and all those whose work I have quoted, exist now in abundance across the whole analytic spectrum. Like a sheet of exposed photographic paper placed in a dish of developer, a new psychotherapeutic paradigm seems to be coming into focus. My label of four dimensionality is simply one attempt to 'fix' it, in order to prepare it for the light of day. Jung applied a multiplicity of related descriptions: transcendent function, objective psyche, pleroma; Winnicott hypothesised a potential space or a third area; Bion spoke of 'faith' and 'O'. While each of these terms carries different connotations they all point to an indefinable core concept; while none wholly conveys the underlying reality, each reflects the differing modes in which this reality has been experienced.

Current therapeutic writings, seminars and debates indicate that more and more practitioners are developing the capacity, where appropriate, to *be* with their patients rather than do things to them; to suffer with them, learn from them, enjoy them, and even be helped by them. There is a greater readiness among therapists and analysts to let their unconscious fuse with that of the patient; temporarily to give up trying to understand and simply share their confusion; even to give up trying to be therapeutic but work from moment to moment, trusting that the patient's own healing capacity can use them for its own purposes. This is a far cry from the omnipotent analyst who took you apart and put you together again. Barely twenty years ago this *via negativa* approach would have been regarded as an abdication of the analytic role. If Freud's remarkable discoveries brought about the first psychological revolution and changed the thinking of the entire twentieth century, Jung must be credited with initiating a second psychological revolution whose impact may not be fully realised until the century to come. In its short history psycho-analysis has moved from drive theory to ego psychology, from ego psychology to object relations theory, and from object relations to individuation. Can it now go beyond? This is hardly a new challenge; in fact it is a very old one. The impulse to transcend the ego goes back to the beginnings of human society, and has been accomplished by a few people in every generation. But in our own historical period, with its capacity to poison and destroy most living forms on the surface of the planet, it has become a necessity.

> At other times and in other civilizations, [the] path of spiritual transformation was confined to a relatively select number of people: now, however, a large proportion of the human race must seek the path of wisdom if the world is to be preserved from the internal and external dangers that threaten it. In this time of violence and disintegration, spiritual vision is not an elitist luxury but vital to our survival.
>
> (Sogyal 1992)

Contemporary society right across the face of the earth is coming dangerously close to breakdown; how much further must it degenerate before a breakthrough can emerge? And what are the forces that might facilitate such a possibility? Depth psychology already possesses the resources to bring to the spiritual quest its powers of clear observation, its accumulated knowledge of pathology, its psychological acumen, its healthy scepticism and its love of truth. It does seem just possible that psychotherapy, by reaching back to its ancient roots in healing and reaching forward to the radical new perspectives of contemporary science, can make its special contribution to the most urgent need of our times.

References

Arden, M. (1985) 'Psychoanalysis and survival', *International Journal of Psychoanalysis*, 66.

Arden, M. (1993) 'Thoughts on the healing process', *International Forum on Psychoanalysis*, 2, Stockholm.

Balint, M. (1958) 'The three areas of the mind', *International Journal of Psychoanalysis*, 39.

Balint, M. (1968) *The Basic Fault*, Tavistock.

Bateson, G. (1972) *Steps to an Ecology of Mind*, Ballantine.

Benvenuto, B. and Kennedy, R. (1986) *The Works of Jacques Lacan: An Introduction*, Free Association Books.

Bion, W.R. (1970) *Attention and Interpretation*, Tavistock.

Bohm, D. (1982) 'The enfolding-unfolding universe: a conversation with David Bohm', Renee Weber. Inc. in K. Wilber (ed.) *The Holographic Paradigm*, Shambhala.

Bowlby, J. (1980) *Attachment and Loss*, Basic Books.

Bromberg, W. (1975) *From Shaman to Psychotherapist*, Regnery.

Brown, J.E. (1981) ' "Mysticism" in the native American tradition', in R. Woods (ed.) *Understanding Mysticism*, Athlone Press.

Campbell, J. (1988) *The Hero with a Thousand Faces*, Paladin.

Capra, F. (1970) *The Tao of Physics*, Wildwood House.

Carotenuto, A. (1984) *A Secret Symmetry*, Routledge & Kegan Paul.

Casement, P.J. (1982) 'Some pressures on the analyst for physical contact during the re-living of early trauma', *International Review of Psychoanalysis*, 9.

Castaneda, C. (1971) *A Separate Reality*, Simon & Schuster.

Chopra, D. (1989) *Quantum Healing*, Bantam Books.

Coltart, N. (1986) 'Slouching towards Bethlehem', in G. Cohon (ed.) *The British School of Psychoanalysis*, Free Association Books.

Conze, E. (1938) *Buddhist Texts*, Dutton.

Cotton, I. (1996) 'God help us', *Independent on Sunday Magazine*, 6 January.

Del Monte, M. (1995) 'Silence and emptiness in the service of healing', *British Journal of Psychotherapy*, 11(3).

Devereux, G. (ed.) (1953) *Psychoanalysis and the Occult*, International Universities Press.

Diekmann, H. (1976) 'Transference and countertransference', *Journal of Analytical Psychology*, 21(1).

Dossey, L. (1985) *Time, Space and Medicine*, Shambhala.

Eigen, M. (1981) 'The area of faith in Winnicott, Lacan, and Bion', *International Journal of Psychoanalysis*, 62.

Eliade, M. (1964) *Shamanism*, Bollinger.

Ellenberger, H. (1970) *The Discovery of the Unconscious*, Basic Books.

Fairbairn, W.R.D. (1952) *Psychoanalytic Studies of the Personality*, Routledge.

Farrell, B. (1981) *The Standing of Psychoanalysis*, Oxford University Press.

Ferenczi, S. (1955) *Final Contributions*, Maresfield.

Field, N. (1989) 'Listening with the body', *British Journal of Psychotherapy*, 5(4).

Field, N. (1992) 'The therapeutic function of altered states', *Journal of Analytical Psychology*, 37(2).

Fisher, S. and Greenberg, R.P. (1985) *The Scientific Credibility of Freud's Theories and Therapy*, Columbia University Press.

Fordham, M. (1969) *Children as Individuals*, Hodder & Stoughton.

Foucault, M. (1981) *The History of Sexuality: Vol. 1*, Penguin.

Freud, S. (1912) 'Recommendations to physicians practising psychoanalysis', SE 12, Hogarth.

Freud, S. (1915) 'The unconscious', SE 14, Hogarth.

Freud, S. (1916–17) *Introductory Lectures on Psychoanalysis*, SE 15–16, Hogarth.

Freud, S. (1918) 'From the history of an infantile neurosis', SE17, Hogarth.

Freud, S. (1919) 'Lines of advance in psycho-analytic therapy', SE 17, Hogarth.

Freud, S. (1923a) *The Ego and the Id*, SE 19, Hogarth.

Freud, S. (1923b) 'A neurosis of demonic possession in the 17th century', SE 4, Hogarth.

Freud, S. (1925) 'Two principles of mental functioning', SE 4, Hogarth.

Freud, S. and Breuer, J. (1895) *Studies on Hysteria*, SE 2, Hogarth.

Govinda, A. (1973) *Foundations of Tibetan Mysticism*, Samuel Weser.

Groesbeck, J. (1989) 'C.G. Jung and the shaman's vision', *Journal of Analytical Psychology*, 34.

Grof, S. (1979) *Realms of the Human Unconscious*, Souvenir Press.

Grotstein, J.S. (1992) 'Reflections on a century of Freud: some paths not chosen', *British Journal of Psychotherapy*, 9(2).

Grunbaum, A. (1944) 'Does psychoanalysis have a future? Doubtful', *Harvard Mental Health Letter*, 11(4).

Guntrip, H. (1968) *Schizoid Phenomena, Object Relations and the Self*, Hogarth.

Harris, G. (1993) 'Projective identification from a Jungian perspective', *Journal of The British Association of Psychotherapists*, 24.

Haule, J. (1990) *Divine Madness*, Shambhala.

Heimann, P. (1960) 'Counter-transference', *British Journal of Medical Psychology*, 33(9).

Hillman, J. (1972) *The Myth of Analysis*, Harper Torchbooks.

Hinshelwood, R.D. (1988) 'Models of demoralisation,' *British Journal of Psychotherapy*, 5(2).

Hinshelwood, R.D. (1991) *A Dictionary of Kleinian Thought*, Free Association Books.

Hollos, I. (1953) 'A summary of Istvan Hollos' Theories' in G. Devereux (ed.) *Psychoanalysis and the Occult*, International Universities Press.

Huxley, A. (1952) *The Devils of Loudun*, Chatto & Windus.

Inge, W.R. (1929) *The Philosophy of Plotinus*, Chatto & Windus.

James, W. (1901) *Varieties of Religious Experience*, Longman.

Jung, C.G. (1944) *Psychology and Alchemy*, CW 12, Routledge.

Jung, C.G. (1954) *The Practice of Psychotherapy*, CW 16, Routledge.

Jung, C.G. (1957) *Psychiatric Studies*, CW 1, Princeton.

Jung, C.G. (1970) *The Structure and Dynamics of the Psyche*, CW 8, Routledge.

Jung, C.G. (1971) *Memories, Dreams, Reflections*, Collins/Routledge.

Kapleau, P. (1967) *The Three Pillars of Zen*, Beacon Press.

Klein, M. (1946) 'Notes on some schizoid mechanisms', *International Journal of Psychoanalysis*, 27.

Klein, M. (1957) *Envy and Gratitude*, Tavistock.

Koestler, A. (1967) *The Ghost in the Machine*, Arkana.

Kohut, H. (1965) 'Forms and transformations of narcissism', *Journal of American Psychoanalytic Assocation*, 14.

Kohut, H. (1977) *The Restoration of the Self*, International Universities Press.

Krishna, G. (1970) *Kundalini*, Shambhala.

Kuras, M.F. (1992) 'Intimacies of the impersonal', *Journal of Analytical Psychology*, 37(4).

Laing, R.D. and Esterson, A. (1964) *Sanity, Madness and the Family*, Tavistock.

Langs, R. (1988) 'Mathematics for psychoanalysis', *British Journal of Psychotherapy*, 5(2).

Levenson, E. (1976) 'A holographic model of psychoanalytic change', *Contemporary Psychoanalysis*, 12.

Malan, D.H. (1973) 'The outcome problem in psychotherapy research', *Archives of General Psychiatry*, 29.

Mann, D. (1994) 'The psychotherapist's erotic subjectivity', *British Journal of Psychotherapy*, 10 (3).

Maslow, A. (1968) *Towards a Psychology of Being*, Van Nostrand.

Mavromatis, A. (1987) *Hypnagogia*, Routledge.

Meltzer, D. (1975) *Explorations in Autism*, Clunie Press.

Meltzer, D. (1979) 'Routine and inspired interpretations', in L. Epstein and A. Feiner (eds) *Countertransference*, Aronson.

Meltzer, D. (1981) 'The Kleinian expansion of Freud's metapsychology', *International Journal of Psychoanalysis*, 62(2).

Meltzer, D. (1992) *The Claustrum*, Clunie Press.

Milner, M. (1987) *The Suppressed Madness of Sane Men*, Tavistock.

Modell, A.H. (1993) *The Private Self*, Harvard University Press.

Mogar, R.E. (1965) 'Current status and future trends in psychedelic research', *Journal of Humanistic Psychology*, 2.

Money-Kyrle, R. (1956) 'Normal countertransference and some of its deviations', *International Journal of Psychoanalysis*, 37.

Norrington, S. (1993) 'Paradox in Winnicott', Lecture to the London Centre for Psychotherapy, 14 September.

Ogden, T.H. (1979) 'On projective identification', *International Journal of Psychoanalysis*, 60.

Ogden, T.H. (1994) 'The analytic third: working with intersubjective clinical facts', *International Journal of Psychoanalysis*, 75(3).

O'Shaughnessy, E. (1981) 'A clinical study of defensive organisation', *International Journal of Psychoanalysis*, 62.

Phillips, A. (1993) 'Contingency for beginners', *Winnicott Studies*, 8.

Pribram, K. (1982) 'What the fuss is all about', in K. Wilber (ed.) *The Holographic Paradigm*, Shambhala.

Rank, O. (1924) *The Trauma of Birth*, Kegan Paul.

Reed, H. (1996) 'Close encounters in the liminal zone: experiments in imaginal communication, Part 1', *Journal of Analytical Psychology*, 41 (1).

Reps, P. (1971) *Zen Flesh, Zen Bones*, Pelican.

Rosen, D.H. (1993) *Transforming Depression*, Putnam.

Rosenfeld, H. (1964) *Psychotic States*, Maresfield.

Rossi, E.L. (1986) 'The ultradian rhythms', *Handbook of Altered States of Consciousness*, Van Nostrand.

Rucker, R. (1994) *The Fourth Dimension*, Penguin.

Rutter, P. (1990) *Sex in the Forbidden Zone*, Mandala.

Rycroft, C. (1985) *Psychoanalysis and Beyond*, Chatto & Windus.

Sabbadini, A. (1991) 'Listening to silence', *British Journal of Psychotherapy*, 7(4).

Samuels, A. (1985) *Jung and the Post-Jungians*, Routledge.

Samuels, A. (1989) *The Plural Psyche*, Routledge.

Sargant, W. (1959) *Battle for the Mind*, Pan Books.

Schwartz-Salant, N. (1984) 'Archetypal factors underlying sexual acting-out in the transference–countertransference process', *Transference and Countertransference*, Chiron.

Schwartz-Salant, N. (1986) 'On the subtle body concept', *The Body in Analysis*, Chiron.

Schwartz-Salant, N. (1988) 'Archetypal foundations of projective identification', *Journal of Analytical Psychology*, 33.

Searles, H. (1965) 'Oedipal love in the countertransference', *Collected Papers on Schizophrenia*, International Universities Press.

Searles, H. (1975) 'The patient as therapist to his analyst', *Counter-transference and Related Subjects*, International Universities Press.

Segal, H. (1986) *The Work of Hanna Segal*, Free Association Books.

Smith, Glass and Miller (1980) *The Benefits of Psychotherapy*, Johns Hopkins University Press.

Sogyal, Rinpoche (1992) *The Tibetan Book of Living and Dying*, Rider.

Spielrein, S. (1994) 'Destruction as the cause of coming into being', *Journal of Analytical Psychology*, 39(2).

Stace, W.T. (1960) *The Teachings of the Mystics*, Mentor.

Stanton, M. (1990) *Sandor Ferenczi*, Free Association Books.

Stein, R. (1973) *Incest and Human Love*, Spring Publications.

Stern, D. (1985) *The Interpersonal World of the Infant*, Basic Books.
Storr, A. (1988) *Solitude*, Flamingo.
Strachey, J. (1959) 'The nature of the therapeutic action of psychoanalysis', *International Journal of Psychoanalysis*, 15.
Suzuki, D. (1962) *The Essentials of Zen Buddhism*, Dutton.
Toynbee, A. (1972) *A Study of History*, Oxford University Press.
Tresan, D. (1996) 'Jungian metapsychology and neurobiological theory', *Journal of Analytical Psychology*, 41(2).
Trungpa, C. (1973) *Cutting Through Spiritual Materialism*, Watkins.
Van Eenwyck, J.R. (1991) 'Archetypes: the strange attractors of the psyche', *Journal of Analytical Psychology*, 36(1).
Watts, A. (1971) *Psychotherapy East and West*, Cape.
Wilber, K. (1977) *The Spectrum of Consciousness*, Theosophical Publishing House.
Wilber, K. (1990) *Eye to Eye*, Shambhala.
Williams, M. (1963) 'The poltergeist man', *Journal of Analytical Psychology*, 8(2).
Winnicott, D.W. (1964) *The Child, the Family and the Outside World*, Tavistock.
Winnicott, D.W. (1965) *The Maturational Process and the Facilitating Environment*, Hogarth.
Winnicott. D.W. (1971) *Playing and Reality*, Penguin Books.
Winnicott, D.W. (1988) 'Communication between infant and mother', *Babies and Their Mothers*, Free Associations.
Yeats, W.B. (1933) *Collected Poems*, Macmillan.
Zinkin, L. (1979) 'Flexibility in analytic technique', in *Technique in Jungian Analysis*, Heinemann.
Zinkin, L. (1987) 'The hologram as a model for analytical psychology', *Journal of Analytical Psychology*, 32(1).

Index